The Future of Business

An Introduction to Artificial Intelligence

David Vandegrift

Table of Contents

Introduction

The purpose of this book

This book is meant to offer an approachable introduction to the ballooning field of Artificial Intelligence. AI is poised to disrupt every major industry in the world. Yet as it stands, accurate and up-to-date information on the field is mostly restricted to the technical practitioner community. Unless you have your PhD in the field, that means that you have to rely on hype-filled misleading news headlines.

The lack of good information on AI for the broader professional community leads to a number of risks. One of the largest is the potential for mistaken expectations. Generic clickbait headlines generate excitement without establishing a timeline for AI's promise and without the necessary detail of *how* AI can be used to solve real problems.

Some have argued that the problem of poorly-informed expectations is one of sensationalism: the headlines are responsible for getting people's hopes up inappropriately. This book is the counter-argument to the claim that the field is being over-hyped. The potential for AI in the near-term really is tremendous. The real issue is that the millions of professionals who can effectuate that potential don't have a full grasp of how to do so. This book is the first step along a journey of discovery for these professionals.

Why this is important

AI is poised to reshape how the world works. Tech companies like Google, IBM, and Microsoft have already made it the core of their development focus. Other companies aren't far behind: McKinsey estimates that total expenditure on AI development and research in 2016 was somewhere in the neighborhood of $30B[1]. They also point to forecasts that say that number could grow as large as $126B by 2025.

I actually believe these estimates understate the true impact of AI, both today and in the future. Just look at Google: machine learning (a large portion of the AI field today) is core to its $89B 2016 revenue and $700B+ market cap.

We are currently in the middle of what is being called an "AI spring", an "AI revolution", or an "AI renaissance". The past few years have seen a massive surge of interest in—and application of—AI technologies in virtually every sector of the economy. And yet, the professional application of AI still significantly lags the rapid progress being made at the cutting edge by scientists and researchers. The changes we've seen in industry today from AI are a small portion of the overall opportunity.

Similar to previous waves of technological disruption, late-adopters of AI technology will be left behind. In an economic context, companies who do not quickly begin experimenting with and adopting AI will face an existential threat sooner rather than later. At an individual level, no professional can afford to be ignorant of the advanced "intelligent" technologies that are replacing the traditional software paradigm.

How to read this book

This book covers a wide array of topics under the broad umbrella of "Artificial Intelligence", from the algorithms used to implement AI to lists of the top AI experts to follow online. While you can read the book from start to finish, you may find it worthwhile to use the Table of Contents to quickly jump around to different sections that interest you.

In general, each chapter of the book will start out with an overview of the subject material and then progressively explore it in more detail. If this is your first exposure to the field of AI, many of the chapters will quickly exceed your level of context and—quite likely—interest. Don't get bogged down in trying to understand each chapter in its entirety. You should progress through each chapter to the extent that you're comfortable, then switch to another chapter as the reading becomes cumbersome. You'll be able to come back to the chapter once your grounding in the field is more established and you'll find the detailed reading much easier.

Why I wrote this book

When I began working as a venture capitalist in 2015, I quickly became enamored with the rising tide of AI companies my firm was evaluating for investment. When given the choice of digging in on a company trying to intelligently unify data across the enterprise or a company bringing decade-old technology to hospitals, the choice seemed obvious to me.

As I set out to learn about AI, I found it incredibly challenging. On one side, there were good high-level resources like the WaitButWhy AI Revolution blog post and *The Singularity is Near*. On the other, arXiv and the blog posts its papers inspired provided a trove of technical knowledge for building cutting edge models. But there was nothing in the middle.

I quickly came to realize that there were virtually no resources for business people (myself included) who were trying to make AI a commercial reality. As rare as the technical skillset to build AI was, the ability to bridge the technical acumen with the real-world demands of business applications basically just didn't exist.

I've spent the past few years learning and honing my understanding of how AI can be applied to real world problems. I've written blog posts and Quora answers, organized Meetups and spoken at conferences; all the while sharpening up frameworks and definitions. This book is the result of those efforts.

Disclaimer

I make no warranty as to the information in this book being up-to-date. I'll do my best to ensure that the information is accurate as of the time of writing, but I have no way of knowing how far in the future you'll be reading this. AI research and application is progressing at light speed, and elements of this book are liable to be out of date nearly as soon as they're written. Think of the information here as a starting point, not as the end-all-be-all source of truth.

In that vein, *please* reach out to me if you find any of the content in this book to be out-of-date, inaccurate, incomplete, or misrepresentative. I will happily update the working version of the book to correct any and all mistakes. Your best bet to reach me is on Twitter, @DavidVandegrift.

Chapter 1

The Definition of AI

"What is artificial intelligence?" For such a simple question, it's astounding how complicated the answer is.

First, you need to understand that artificial intelligence is an unregulated term. There is no central group to set a standard definition or regulate the usage of the term.

Second, artificial intelligence isn't a specific thing. It's a categorical structure with a lot of different topics underneath it. It's best identified by a "you'll know it when you see it" type of definition that can't be easily looked up in a dictionary.

Third, artificial intelligence isn't even really a scientific or technical term. As opposed to a field like biology, which does have a fairly particular scientific meaning, artificial intelligence is more of a layman's term. It's a casual reference to a broad collection of ideas, some of which are technical and some of which aren't.

According to Merriam Webster[2], AI is either "a branch of computer science dealing with the simulation of intelligent behavior in computers" (AI the field) or "the capability of a machine to imitate intelligent human behavior" (AI the capability). The key term in each of those definitions that makes this question so difficult is "intelligence", which is—of course— at the root of the term "*artificial* intelligence".

One of the reasons that AI is unlikely to have a fixed, strict definition any time soon is because *intelligence* doesn't have such a definition. Scientists disagree about all kinds of questions around this topic: How do you measure intelligence in humans?

Is there only one kind of intelligence? Are animals intelligent? *Can* animals be intelligent? Can machines be intelligent? In practice, these seemingly simple questions often quickly devolve into philosophical debates around just what it means to be intelligent.

If we can't decide for a certainty what intelligence actually is, we're doomed to never have a really solid definition for artificial intelligence. But to some extent, that's actually okay. The term "artificial intelligence" is only useful to the extent that we can all agree on what it means when we use it. Because the term is so ill-defined, it is often practical to minimize reliance on use of the term entirely. Or at the very least, use it only in specific contexts where the likely interpretation can be reasonably guessed ahead of time.

Despite—or perhaps because of—the lack of agreement around what AI really is, a number of proposed "standard" definitions have arisen. I'll explain a few of the more popular ones further.

Cognitive computing

There are a number of terms that have been pushed forward as alternatives to "artificial intelligence", presumably in an attempt to avoid all of this conflict and confusion entirely. For the most part these terms have only *added* to the noise, but they are worth considering anyway. One is "machine intelligence", which as far as I can tell is synonymous with AI and all of the nuances of its many definitions.

Another is "cognitive computing". This one is interesting because it connotes a specific definition of AI that is close to how many people use it in practice.

Cognitive computing, as a term, is unofficially "owned" by technology giant IBM. They use the term exclusively when referring to their intelligent offerings (broadly branded under Watson); "artificial intelligence" is nowhere to be found in their marketing materials. Interestingly, they tend to shy away from defining the term and sketching out how it's different from regular artificial intelligence, at least formally or in writing.

While there is no standard definition for cognitive computing, there is a general bent among most: it's the field that involves using computers to mimic human thought. This is also an interesting definition for AI overall, as it is broadly how many people think of the field. While defining human thought versus animal intelligence versus plain calculation is a sticky discussion all on its own, the cognitive definition of AI at least lands close to the heart of the topic for many.

The AI Effect

The AI Effect is a restatement of Tesler's Theorem[3], "Artificial Intelligence is whatever hasn't been done yet." According to Tesler, his actual statement was that "Intelligence is whatever machines haven't done yet." In other words, according to the AI Effect, AI is defined as any problem that computers cannot yet solve.

The AI Effect is more a social or psychological phenomenon than a technical one. The idea is that any level of machine-performed computation was once thought of as AI, from adding two numbers to defeating grandmasters in chess. Indeed, there was a time when a simple pocket calculator from today would have been considered the pinnacle of AI. As that type of calculation became commonplace, people stopped thinking of it as a sign of intelligence.

Once a computer solves some problem, the general public points to some tidbit that "proves" the accomplishment wasn't the result of "true" AI. Deep Blue's chess victory over Kasparov is a great case study: chess skill was considered to be a direct reflection of human intelligence (in the Western world) until computers became better than humans. Now, it is common for people to point to Deep Blue's "brute force" method of move calculation as a sign that it's not "real" AI.

An interesting outcome of the AI Effect as a definition of AI is that AI is determined by its *outcome*, as opposed to its composition. In human terms, a person could have the fastest, largest brain in the world, yet not be considered intelligent if they never apply their mind to a task that others recognize as novel or meaningful. Of course, that's perhaps not that far off from how our society actually *does* view human intelligence.

Another—more frustrating—outcome of the AI Effect is that AI has no fixed definition. Instead, AI is a moving goal post that becomes progressively more restrictive as more advanced software is developed that can perform ever-more-impressive feats.

While it would seem that this lack of a fixed definition (from the perspective of specific technology) would limit the usefulness of the AI Effect perspective in practice, that has not really happened. Leading "AI" conferences or publications actually *have* shifted their focus over time. Expert systems may have been covered as cutting-edge AI in the mid 70s by the very same (or similar) groups to the ones that now dismiss them as not being AI at all. As technology progresses, specific classes of models (deep neural networks, for instance) often end up with their own dedicated communities and events that eschew usage of—or concern with—the broader AI terminology entirely.

It is worth noting that in practice, the AI Effect may be a poor definition for the corporate use case. You can imagine the potential costs of rallying an organization around a major AI initiative, only to turn around and tell the organization that the implementation is not AI at all once it is complete.

AI as ML

An informal definition of AI that has gained much traction over the past few years is the view that machine learning and artificial intelligence are perfectly synonymous. That is, there is no type of artificial intelligence that is not machine learning.

The cause for this definition's popularity is not difficult to guess: almost all of the advancements in the broad field of AI that have lead to the recent surge in overall interest have been the result of machine learning work (primarily deep learning, which I'll define next). In comparison, non-ML types of intelligent software like expert systems or linear programming really haven't progressed all that much in this short time period. As a result, many onlookers—particularly those new to the field—might reasonably say that work in machine learning is the only type of recent AI work that really matters. It is not much of a stretch from there to conclude, "ML is the only type of AI".

However, the "AI = ML" definition falls short in some clear ways. One is that most people would not consider a simple application of some of the most basic machine learning models to be artificial intelligence. Many business analysts are familiar with the spreadsheet function to fit a line to a scatter plot of data points. The fitting of such a line might rely on the machine learning model of linear regression. If the analyst were to show their manager the chart exulting over their mastery of artificial intelligence, the manager might (understandably) be nonplussed.

Another flaw with the definition particular to the business world is that the *how* of an intelligent program is often completely irrelevant in the face of the *what*. To the diagnostic imaging company, a model that can accurately and quickly detect a cancerous growth may be very lucrative. Whether that model uses convolutional neural networks or a hand-tuned set of rules is mostly irrelevant.

AI as DL

An "evolved" form of the "AI = ML" definition is that Artificial Intelligence is actually only a *subset* of machine learning called deep learning, and nothing else. Later sections of this book will spend significant time on what deep learning is and why it is important; for now, just know that it is an advanced type of machine learning that is significantly more difficult to implement than basic models and can produce better results on many complex problems.

Restricting the definition of AI to deep learning circumvents the problem I described previously: that a basic linear regression line fitting on a scatter plot wouldn't be considered AI by most people. In some ways, "AI = DL" is a combination of "AI = ML" and the AI Effect because deep learning is simply the most recent type of machine learning that the technology crowd hasn't grown accustomed to yet.

However, "AI = DL" doesn't address the business concerns of the "AI = ML" definition. In fact, it complicates them. In terms of volume of projects, deep learning is much less practical for business use cases than the rest of the machine learning toolkit (at least today).

AI must learn

Many in the field rely on various definitions of AI that require that any kind of AI software must learn. These definitions fall along the lines of "a program that solves problems by learning" or "a program that makes predictions about the future by learning from the past".

While there may not technically be a difference between this definition and the "AI = ML" definition (depending on how that second definition is applied), this definition is potentially more restrictive in one key way.

Most people would consider the AlphaGo program that defeated Lee Sedol and "conquered" the game of Go to be artificial intelligence, including most adherents to the "AI = ML" definition. That is because AlphaGo was a system based on deep neural networks that were trained through reinforcement learning. However, it is important to note that the software program that actually played Lee Sedol *was not learning*. The learning capabilities of AlphaGo had been turned off before the match began.

According to those who define AI as learning software, AlphaGo was not AI during that match. While that definition of AI may be as valid as any in an objective sense, it is even more poorly suited to a business context than the "AI = ML" definition, as it is not only completely divorced from the outcome of the software, but also relies on a specific technical mechanism that doesn't affect the behavior of the software in any meaningful way.

The Turing test (AGI)

The Turing test is probably the most widely recognized (implied) definition of AI in the general public. The test, developed by Alan Turing in 1950, is relatively straightforward: a piece of software must try to convince a human observer that the software is—in fact—a human. If the software succeeds in fooling the observer "judge", then it has passed the Turing test.

While it cannot be rigorously proven, most people believe that any software that can pass the Turing test must be generally as intelligent as a human. This gives rise to three important terms that are at the crux of many long-sighted debates around AI:

- **Artificial Narrow Intelligence (ANI)** - AI that performs a single task or modest collection of cognitive tasks quite well; perhaps better than a human can.
- **Artificial General Intelligence (AGI)** - AI that can perform any cognitive task at least as well as a human can.
- **Artificial Super Intelligence (ASI)** - AI that can perform any cognitive task substantially better than a human can.

All AI to-date is still in the realm of ANI. While software can do many things better than humans can (like play chess or recognize faces), there are still many cognitive tasks on which computers vastly underperform almost all humans. Additionally, AI software today is quite bad at adapting from one task to another. As of time of writing, there is no publicly-announced software that can both beat a human at chess and recognize faces with more accuracy.

The Turing test definition of AI says that AI and AGI are synonymous: no piece of software can be called AI unless it performs generally as well as a human across tasks. This definition is similar to the AI Effect definition in that it sets a future goal post: no software today can be considered AI. However, unlike the AI Effect definition, the Turing test definition has a fixed technology in mind and has a wide variety of proposed tests for evaluating whether a program qualifies as AI or not.

Similar to the "AI must learn" definition, the Turing test definition of AI is not very practical for the business world. The field of AI is a reality for the business professional today, and it is not sufficient to cut short every discussion on the topic by saying that we are still years or decades away from the invention of AI.

Russell and Norvig's definition

Although it is not particularly well-suited to the business world, it is worth mentioning another commonly-cited definition of AI. This one comes from *Artificial Intelligence: A Modern Approach* by Stuart Russell and Peter Norvig. As this book is sometimes referred to as the "AI bible", it has shaped many practitioners' thinking on the field.

In their book[4], Russell and Norvig define AI as concerned with "the designing and building of intelligent agents that receive percepts from the environment and take actions that affect that environment". In business applications, AI typically does not take the form of an agent (with notable exceptions: for instance, customer service). This definition is most closely related to the fields of reinforcement learning and robotics.

How to proceed

It is worth noting that this book stops short of proposing a specific definition for AI. As a reminder, the purpose of this book is to prepare the business professional for an AI-centric world. For better or worse, it is unlikely that the broad population will ever agree on a single definition. As such, the savvy professional should be aware of the various perspectives on AI and should be able to tailor their communication according to the perspective of their audience.

Assuming you don't want to get bogged down in theoretical and philosophical debates when discussing AI, it may be best to avoid significant efforts to define AI at all. Instead, focus on the *how* and *why* of AI-related business initiatives. The diagnostic imaging company from before should talk about speeding up and improving cancerous growth diagnosis, rather than "becoming an AI company".

An advantage of spending more time and energy on the substance of the problem than the definition is that it decreases the opportunity for misaligned expectations. Applying convolutional neural networks to object detection in images is a fairly concrete and reasonably-well-understood problem. It is much easier for stakeholders to get their minds around than some abstract push to "use more AI".

If the various schools of thought on what constitutes AI *is* particularly interesting to you, please note that this chapter provided only a very cursory exploration of a select few approaches. Please do seek out other resources for a more thorough treatment. The "Philosophy of artificial intelligence" article on Wikipedia is a great starting point. You can also refer to the Further Resources section at the end of this book.

Chapter 2

The History of AI

In approaching the field of artificial intelligence today, it is helpful to have an understanding and appreciation of how the field got to its present state. That context lays the groundwork for a meaningful definition of AI, provides validity for the robustness of the field as the product of centuries of work, and establishes historical precedent for the possibilities of advancement in the field over time.

This chapter seeks to lay that groundwork. For such a young field, the history of AI is surprisingly rich. This chapter just covers the most significant of the milestones and draws out some of the connections to navigating the AI landscape from a business context today.

If this is a topic that interests you, please consider seeking out other resources that cover the field's history in more detail. Wikipedia provides an uncharacteristically fantastic introduction. You can also refer to the Further Resources section at the end of this book.

Precursors to AI

While to most casual observers it may seem that AI is a purely 20th century invention, the reality is a bit more complex. AI is more a social creation: a construct of humans' efforts to understand their place in the universe and what separates them from the rest of creation. As such, the roots of AI are as old as humans themselves; far predating the current computation technology we've used to realize the vision.

Humans have been envisioning artificial creations that exhibit cognition since prehistoric times. Some of the earliest recorded references include the Greeks' Hephaestus creating gold automotons to guard a palace, Aristotle postulating that slavery could one day be abolished with the advent of mechanical laborers, and an invention of Al-Jazari composed of automated "musicians" floating on a lake.

Throughout most of history, these intelligent creations were mostly driven by mechanical means: complex gears, air, and hydraulics. This is a testament to AI as a concept being greater than the current paradigm we understand. Societies envisioned AI long before they had the digital and silicon substrate that we use to write software today.

The emergence of statistical analysis

The earliest seeds of a mathematical approach to creating artificial intelligence can be found in the earliest days of the field of statistics. The roots of that field are often traced to the 1600s, when early methods were developed for the census of human population. The field steadily progressed through the 1600s and 1700s, with the method of least squares (a way of minimizing a model's error) being invented in the very early days of the 1800s. Least squares is of note because it is still commonly used as a method to reduce the error of machine learning models today.

In 1763, Thomas Bayes invented an equation for a model to update itself as new information comes in. That equation was generalized into Bayes' theorem, which provides a general equation for predicting the probability of a given event based on the knowledge of a set of other conditions. Bayes' theorem is at the heart of many predictive models in the field of machine learning.

While these early advances in statistics lie at the core of machine learning, it is worth noting that they were developed entirely independently of any concept of applying them *with machines*. It probably goes without saying, but every model in machine learning *can* theoretically be applied by hand, without the use of a machine at all. As such, the field could—in some ways—be more accurately referred to as mathematical learning.

This is highly relevant as you consider the various definitions of AI. Vanishingly few people would consider a hand-written regression model to be AI. And yet, the only difference between that model and the one performed by your spreadsheet application is that the one is the result of your biological nerves and muscles while the other is the product of electricity in silicon (namely, the machine). In other words, the *machine* truly is an integral part of machine learning and artificial intelligence more broadly. The math alone is not enough.

One potential line of thinking takes you to a (partial) definition of AI that was not explored in the previous chapter. Specifically, that machine learning is not a perfect subset of AI at all. If a hand-written regression model is not AI and the only difference between that and a computer's regression model is that the second is performed by a machine, then you must believe that difference is fundamental to the definition of AI. If you don't, then it follows that machine learning models don't necessarily need to be AI: that a basic regression model can just be math that doesn't cross the definitional threshold.

The birth of modern AI

AI, as it is practiced today, is often traced back to the conceptual invention of the "artificial neuron" in 1943 by Warren McCulloch and Walter Pitts. In a move that you will see repeated throughout AI history, McCulloch and Pitts took inspiration from the greatest intelligence in the world they knew of: the human brain. They sought to replicate the functionality of the base unit of the brain (the neuron) using mathematics.

It is no coincidence that this earliest example of modern AI coincides with the beginning of the rise of the modern computer (ENIAC, one of the earliest computers, was invented in 1946). As machines were invented that could perform more and more complex computations, the researchers began to wonder how to push the capabilities of the computers as quickly and as far as possible. The 1940s kicked off a wave of interest in computers for general computation overall, but also in computers simulating human cognition. This is—depending on your definition—the field of artificial intelligence.

As mentioned previously, a famous step forward in defining the field of AI was made in 1950 with Alan Turing's invention of a test to assess the intelligence of a machine (now known as the Turing test). Turing's idea was that one could test the intelligence of a machine by having it try to fool a human judge into thinking the machine was a fellow human. While we're still far away from being able to pass the Turing test, the test provides a standard that AGI researchers can aspire to. It has also spawned a number of variations that can loosely measure the progress toward passing the final test. For example, one such variation instructs the human judge that the person they're speaking with is an adolescent non-native English speaker.

The field of artificial intelligence research (by that name) was born in 1956 at a conference that took place over the course of the summer at Dartmouth. Attendees filtered in and out over the weeks, but at the core were AI legends like Allen Newell, Herbert Simon, John McCarthy, Marvin Minsky, and Arthur Samuel.

This first meeting of the minds to formalize the field of artificial intelligence was more a brainstorming session than a concrete problem solving workshop. Although there was no concrete progress as a result of the event, it was a harbinger of a period of near-unbridled optimism. This is illustrated by the below quotes from prominent researchers at the time:

- Herbert Simon, 1957: "There are now in the world machines that think, that learn, and that create. Moreover, their ability to do these things is going to increase rapidly until in a visible future the range of problems they can handle will be coextensive with the range to which the human mind has been applied."[5]
- I.J. Good, 1959: "My own guess for the time it will take to develop a really useful artificial brain is 20 years multiplied or divided by 1 ½"[6]

- Marvin Minsky, 1961: "I am very optimistic about the eventual outcome of the work on machine solution of intellectual problems. Within our lifetime machines may surpass us in general intelligence."[7]

These early predictions—and many others like them—did not pan out exactly as was envisioned in the earliest days of AI. Today, nearly 60 years later, there is still no clear line of sight to a computer that can rival the human brain in general problem solving ability. These predictions were the seeds for a running joke in the AI community that regardless of when you ask a researcher, they will always say that AGI is 20 years away. Indeed, one of the more commonly cited dates for a current prediction of achieving AGI is the year 2040 (about 21 years from time of writing).

The Dartmouth conference was also the stage for another famous early step forward in the field of AI. Allen Newell and Herbert Simon used the gathering as an opportunity to present Logic Theorist, a piece of software that they had spent the previous year developing. The program made use of symbolic logic to prove fundamental math theorems. In fact, it would eventually prove 38 of the 52 theorems in *Principia Mathematica*. Some of its proofs where even more practical or elegant than the existing predominant proofs.

Logic Theorist is often called the first AI program. Ironically, it did not make much of a splash at the Dartmouth conference when it was presented. Still, Logic Theorist can be seen as the first of a wave of AI software developed between the mid 50s and early 70s.

The mid 1970s saw a dip in interest in the field that came to be known as the first AI winter. Although a massive amount of progress had been made in the field, some of the earliest "20 years out" predictions were clearly falling short: researchers were no closer to mimicking the human brain. The optimism of the early years attracted a massive amount of criticism from all sides, including from fellow researchers frustrated when the field did not progress as quickly as expected.

One of the largest causes of the first AI winter was the inability for hardware to perform the necessary computations.

While processing power was improving extra-linearly according to Moore's Law (roughly doubling every two years), the compute necessary to rival the human brain was vastly underestimated. Indeed, computers today are still nowhere close to having the capacity to perform the calculations that the human brain does: the largest artificial neural networks ever built are less than a thousandth the size of a human brain.

Another major cause was the fundamental limitations of logic-based systems like Logic Theorist. While perfect for mathematical proofs, they did not prove versatile enough to model most real-world environments.

The first AI winter, however, was short-lived. The 1980s saw mass corporate adoption of AI models called "expert system"—essentially a manually-programmed set of rules that would allow computers to make decisions. These expert systems could be incredibly complex, leading to a phenomenon known as "emergent behavior": outcomes that did not appear to be pre-programmed at all.

Although the knowledge-based approach was not invented in the 80s, it took time to make its way from the academic arena to the business world. In 1980, the Digital Equipment Corporation implemented an expert system that saved the company tens of millions of dollars per year. The system automated the company's hardware design specifications and became a widely-regarded case study. This rang in a new period of corporations implementing similar expert systems with significant economic impact. Expert systems still play a vital role in the software world today, though it has fallen out of vogue to refer to them as a type of artificial intelligence.

Unfortunately, just as with the first AI boom, expectations exceeded the short-term potential of the field. When real-world results did not match the hype, corporations and investors became disillusioned with the field entirely. This lead to the second AI winter, which began in the late 80s. The end of the second AI winter is a subject of debate, but some would argue that it continued all the way to the present state of rekindled excitement around 2015.

It is worth noting that while the world's interest and excitement around AI has followed a bit of a roller coaster since the 1950s, the underlying progress in the field has been fairly steady. Some of this is directly attributable to the hardware industry: the computing power of silicon has continued to (more or less) follow Moore's Law since the invention of the field of AI, as the demand for computers has largely been independent of the field.

Even in relatively depressed years of interest, there have been significant milestones in the field. While the late 90s were not a particularly ebullient time for AI practitioners, IBM successfully "conquered" the game of chess in 1997 when Deep Blue defeated Garry Kasparov. While many alive at the time will remember this crowning achievement, the disappointment from the first two hype cycles of AI proved to be too much of a dampener to reignite widespread interest in the field at the time.

AI today

As a whole, the 90s and the first decade of the 2000's were relatively quiet in terms of major leaps forward for the field of AI. As always, research progressed steadily. However, for the most part even dedicated researchers in the field avoided the term "artificial intelligence" and it was not a hot area of investment in the business world.

The first signs of change began in 2011, when IBM's Watson competed—and won—on Jeopardy. IBM's question-answering agent defeated some of the top Jeopardy champions of all time. Coming off the success of its prime-time debut, IBM doubled down on the Watson platform and invested heavily in the development of its "cognitive computing" solutions. It was the first of the tech giants to publicly plant its flag in AI as the future of software.

The field was relatively quiet for a couple of years after Watson's big splash and many pointed to another over-inflation of AI expectations. That turned around quickly.

One of the first major breakthroughs of the current AI era was on a competition called ImageNet. The ImageNet competition was launched in 2010 with the goal of using software to correctly identify objects in images. That first year, the winner of the competition correctly identified 72% of the objects. From there, progress was rapid: by 2015 the winner surpassed human-level accuracy with a score of 96% by making use of convolutional neural networks. For the first time, AI was showing super-human performance in a domain that required rich information processing about the world around it.

Since the triumph in the ImageNet competition, there have been dozens of other achievements big and small. In early 2016, in a widely-covered match reminiscent of Deep Blue's victory over Kasparov, a computer program called AlphaGo defeated Lee Sedol, one of the top Go players in the world. Just months before this victory, some AI experts still believed that a super-human Go program was at least a decade away.

The AlphaGo story is a particularly interesting one. In 2014 Google acquired a UK-based company called DeepMind for something on the order of $500M. At that time, DeepMind had yet to make a single dollar in revenue (or even really a product). The company had established its reputation by creating software that played old Atari games particularly well. While the acquisition may have seemed questionable at the time, it may go down as one of the savviest corporate AI plays in history.

DeepMind is the developer of the AlphaGo program that conquered Go. It has since created a superior version called Alpha Zero, which is substantially better than the original Go champion AI. As if that were not enough, Alpha Zero is now also the top chess player in the world.

To prove that this technology had applications outside of games and mind exercises, Google turned DeepMind's technology onto its own data centers in 2016. The AI evaluated a wide variety of complex conditions (weather, data center architecture, usage of various server clusters, etc.) and optimized the cooling system, one of the primary uses of energy in that environment. With this single application, Google achieved annual cost savings roughly equivalent to its original purchase price of DeepMind just two years prior.

Just in early 2019, OpenAI—another AI corporate powerhouse—developed an AI program that defeated the world's top human players at popular eSports game Dota 2. This marked the first time that computers had ever successfully bested humans in a modern strategy-based video game.

The past few years have seen AI achieving super-human level performance on a variety of other interesting tasks: facial recognition, emotion detection, and some varieties of poker. At time of writing in mid 2019, there is significant discussion around whether or not AI has achieved human-level performance on both voice-to-text (Siri understanding you) and text-to-voice (Siri speaking to you). The main issue in declaring either of those problems solved is primarily around the lack of a standard benchmark; for all realistic purposes, there now exist programs that can do each at least as well as humans.

The massive advances in AI in the past few years are fascinating: the kinds of achievements that would have stood out across a decade of research in previous years are now occurring on a nearly monthly basis. For all the practitioners urging caution in this most recent hype cycle due to fears of a return to an AI winter, it's impossible to deny the massive progress the excitement and attention on the field has driven in just a couple of short years.

While a large number of factors have combined to lead to the current surge in AI progress and excitement, there are a few key elements that stand out from the rest. The first is that nearly all of the major achievements previously listed are the result of models built using deep neural networks. Deep neural networks will be explored in more detail in the chapter on AI Technologies, but the basic idea is that they're mathematical models that were specifically developed to mimic the problem-solving ability of the human brain (hence their name).

The type of deep neural networks that perform well on ImageNet are a particularly interesting case study. The model, known as a convolutional neural network, is inspired by a neurobiological understanding of the human optic nerve and eye. Perhaps unsurprisingly, convolutional neural networks have proven remarkably good at image processing problems. What is more surprising is that they've also shown a lot of promise in other forms of rich media processing, like audio and text.

Of course, deep neural networks are not a particularly recent invention. They trace their roots back to the 60s and all of the theoretical foundations were in place by the mid 80s. What really enabled deep neural networks to begin dominating the field in recent years is the steady progress of hardware.

In other words, Moore's Law finally allowed processors to enable deep neural networks to realize the potential for the field of artificial intelligence that had been promised for decades. In fact, relatively few of the advances in recent years are considered to be particularly novel from a conceptual standpoint; for the most part, it's just the result of ever-more-powerful hardware behind relatively straightforward deep neural networks.

That phenomenon (that faster hardware has enabled much of the progress we see today) has led many to minimize the accomplishments of the researchers pioneering AI advances. This minimization is unfair: even with all the compute power in the world, building out a deep neural network based system to solve real-world problems is far from trivial. And in reality, there is a fair amount of model engineering beyond simply "throw a deep neural network at it".

Much of the pessimism around recent developments also ignores some of the truly fascinating work being done at the forefront of the research community. While DeepMind's application of deep neural networks to reinforcement learning may not be completely novel, it is still incredibly advanced and has led to undeniable progress on several previously unsolved problems. Beyond reinforcement learning, recent years have seen mind-blowing advancements in sub-fields like one shot learning (empowering deep neural networks to achieve results similar to today's models with an order of magnitude less data) and generative models.

There are several sections later in the book dedicated to generative adversarial networks and their potential for impact on the world. By themselves, they should silence many of those who argue that no meaningful AI has been invented since the 1980s (generative adversarial networks were first proposed by Ian Goodfellow in 2014).

Chapter 3

A Framework for Understanding AI

When I first began evaluating AI companies for potential investment as a venture capitalist, I was incredibly confused by just what it meant for a startup to *be* an AI company. I spent a lot of time understanding what AI itself was and what people were referring to when they referenced the field of AI; after a lot of reading, I mostly came up with the various definitions you can find in "The Definition of AI" chapter in this book.

But knowing the various definitions of AI didn't really get me much closer to being able to evaluate what made an AI company. All of the terms were getting jumbled up: computer vision, robotics, convolutional neural networks. I would receive a pitch deck full of these terms and had no ability to distinguish what was real and what was just hype or vaporware.

I hear these same problems from a lot of people who are looking to begin exploring the field of AI in depth. There are so many various sub-fields and specific technologies that it is incredibly difficult for the casual observer to understand what any given company or group of people is working on.

A big contributor to this issue is that there is no well-defined framework organizing the field. After a bit of exposure, people can generally point to the difference between a deep neural network and a logistic regression model. But then how does that compare to natural language processing? Or anomaly detection?

The ex-consultant in me couldn't live in a world with no clear framework. So I created one. As I learned more about the various areas of artificial intelligence, I incorporated them into this mental model. If they didn't fit neatly, I adjusted the model such that it encompassed everything I came across.

Technologies, Applications, and Use Cases. Oh my!

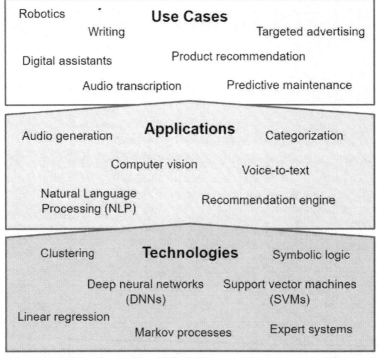

A framework for understanding AI, including non-exhaustive examples for each major category

The first step to understanding where everything fits in the field of AI is to break it into three major categories: **technologies**, **applications**, and **use cases**.

- **Technologies** - The fundament of AI. These are the mathematical and algorithmic models that actually do the work. AI technologies include models like expert systems, linear regression, support vector machines, and deep neural networks.

- **Applications** - So-named because they involve *applying* AI technologies to some kind of problem. AI applications involve no models or algorithms on their own, but will still generally not be recognizable by name to the average non-technical person. Applications fall into sub-categories like natural language processing, computer vision, and voice-to-text.
- **Use cases** - Actual usage of AI technologies and applications for real-world problems. This is the area of AI that is directly visible to most non-technical people. AI use cases include autonomous vehicles, digital assistants like Siri, and product recommendation engines (as popularized by Amazon and Netflix).

Any specific mention of AI you come across should fall into one of these major categories. Understanding which category to place a given type of AI in is critical to being able to navigate the overall field of AI fluently.

It is worth noting that a piece of AI that falls in the "use cases" category will also rely on items from the "applications" and "technologies" categories. Similarly, an item in the "applications" category will rely on one or more "technologies". That is to say, each category builds on the ones that come before it. Technologies are the basis of AI. Applications make use of technologies to solve problems. Use cases make applications practical to the real world.

With that in mind, you can generally point to how a given real-world AI falls into each of the categories. As an example, look at Netflix's movie recommendation functionality. The "use case" is movie recommendations for a Netflix user based on their previously stated preferences. The "application" is recommendation engines (recommendation engines can also recommend things like physical products, articles or books to read, or just about anything else). The "technologies" likely include several machine learning models working in concert. These are likely classification models, like logistic regression, and random forest. As such, when classifying Netflix's use of AI, you might say that it's a movie recommender, a recommendation engine, and a random forest model all at once!

The following three chapters explore each of these categories in more detail, including a fairly comprehensive list of the types of artificial intelligence that fall into each bucket. You are not expected to remember this classification system or the items that belong to it perfectly. Rather, it is most useful to become familiar with the overall framework and develop the skill to place a given piece of AI within it.

It is best to treat the following three chapters as 1) an introduction and exploration of this conceptual framework and 2) a reference guide as you come across implementations of AI in the wild.

Chapter 4

AI Technologies

AI technologies are made up of software-level models and algorithms. They are the type of AI that is least visible to the average non-technical person, but are commensurately vital to the value of the field as a whole. Historically, the technologies were the area of AI least approachable to the average business person. While that may have been acceptable in the era of expert systems when everything was done manually, it is now important for anyone who will be making business decision involving AI (which will be just about everyone) to have an understanding of the technologies underlying the field.

For instance, one probable decision a professional might need to make is what language translation software to purchase to facilitate communication with international customers. While comparing performance on an objective benchmark is the best approach, there is no good third party benchmark and running the test on every single option out there is prohibitively expensive. The AI-savvy professional could run a first pass filter on solutions by removing any software that doesn't make use of either a convolutional neural network or a recurrent neural network, as all top machine translation solutions today tend to rely on one of these two models.

As you have likely gathered from previous chapters in this book and your exposure to the field more broadly, there is a major divide within the category of AI technologies between machine learning models and the rest of the AI models. Sometimes these other models are referred to as "Good Old

Fashioned AI". Here we will refer to them as "static" models, indicating that they do not change over time in response to new data, as a machine learning model would.

Static models

As the name of the sub-category implies, static models do not change over time. They are manually programmed by humans (for now) according to a fixed set of rules. As long as the same inputs are fed into the model, the outputs will always be the same.

Other than their difference from machine learning models, there is no clear definition for what constitutes a static AI model. Very few people would consider a single simple if/else block of code to be AI, yet at their core even the most advanced expert systems are just combinations of such if/else blocks. You would be hard pressed to put your finger on just how many if/else conditions you would need before the program becomes AI. Actually, believers in the "AI = ML" definition of AI would argue that there is no such number.

Below is a non-exhaustive list of static AI models with brief descriptions.

Symbolic logic

If you read the chapter on the history of AI, you may recognize symbolic logic from the brief mention of the first AI program, Logic Theorist. Symbolic logic relies on modeling the world as a set of symbols and interactions between the symbols (arithmetic, for instance, is a form of symbolic logic). Symbolic logic dominated in the early days of computing, between the 1940s and 1960s. Early success with symbolic logic drove a lot of the earliest excitement about the field of AI, but it has relatively little relevance to the business world today.

Expert system

```
if object.has_fur():
    if object.has_tail():
        object.type = 'Guinea pig'
    else:
        object.type = 'cat'
else:
    object.type = 'human'
```

An example of a very simple expert system

Expert systems also made an appearance in the chapter on the history of AI, as the dominant model of the second period of excitement around AI in the 1980s. Expert systems (also called knowledge-based systems) codify human knowledge into a computer program. Tactically, this typically looks like coding a set of rules manually in a series of if/else blocks.

Expert systems probably contribute more to the confusion around the definition of AI than any other model. Because they are programmed manually and there is so much variation between specific models, it becomes difficult to define exactly what constitutes an expert system and what is just plain old programming.

Expert systems abound in the real world today; finding specific examples is difficult because they're integrated into virtually every major software application to some extent. That's a contributor to the confusion: a lot of people new to the AI hype struggle to understand how something so ubiquitous in their software could be in the same field as the mystical deep neural networks they keep hearing about.

Decision tree

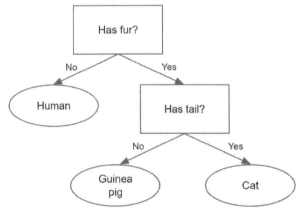

An example of a simple decision tree

A decision tree is a set of comparisons applied to an input to reach a variety of predetermined outcomes. Each comparison leads to a branch, which may have more comparisons to be made. This series of branchings leads to the "tree" portion of the name.

Decision trees are not mutually exclusive with expert systems. Rather, they can be thought of as a particular way of structuring the logic of an expert system.

It is important to note that when you come across the term "decision tree", it is often in the context of machine learning, *not* a static model. Technically, machine learning applied to decision trees is called "decision tree learning". However, in practice, most models called decision trees are actually not static models at all. For the most part, static decision trees will just be referred to as expert systems.

Semantic graph

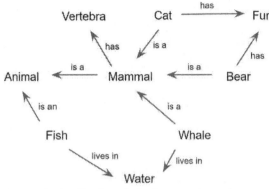

A visualization of a basic semantic graph

Semantic graphs are more a method of storing information than a model for solving problems or making decisions. Still, they are an important technology for most AI applications dealing with natural language understanding.

Semantic graphs describe the relationships between entities, topics, or ideas. They are structured in the form of an information graph: each node of the graph representing a topic and each edge of the graph representing some form of relationship between two nodes.

The most famous example of a semantic graph is Knowledge Graph, Google's effort to document the structure and interrelationship of things in the world. When you see results returned directly to a Google search—rather than as a link to another website—often the result has been retrieved from Knowledge Graph. Google's Knowledge Graph is so popular that "knowledge graph" has become a common name for semantic graphs in the generic sense.

Optimization

Optimization is an entire field of mathematics and computer science unto itself. In fact, it is at the core of machine learning. Still, it is worth considering optimization models as their own class of static AI models.

Optimization is simply maximizing or minimizing a function. Despite its conceptual simplicity, it is incredibly powerful. It is behind most routing software (like Uber and FedEx) and most scheduling software (useful for restaurant shifts or airline flights).

While the outcomes of optimization models are often impressive enough to be considered AI, interestingly there is relatively little overlap between the broader AI research community and the optimization community. Most optimization practitioners are not particularly bothered over the question of whether or not their work qualifies as AI.

Statistical model

While many statistical models on their own don't cross the threshold to be considered AI, there are certain types of statistical models that fall squarely in the domain. For instance, the statistical models commonly used for part of speech recognition in natural language processing are an important part of that broader AI application.

As with static AI models overall, the lack of a clear definition on what statistical models qualify for the AI label means that you're often left simply making the judgment call on a case by case basis.

It can be difficult to categorize static AI because of the lack of clear definitions in the field. In practice, often the best approach is "you know it when you see it". If software appears to have sufficiently advanced problem solving that reminds you of human cognition, yet doesn't actually learn, then it may be a good candidate for being a static AI model.

As mentioned, the heyday of static models was in the past. This most recent AI boom has been largely focused on machine learning models. Given that, it would be reasonable to think that you might be able to ignore static models entirely. But you do so at your own risk.

Although they're not typically referred to as AI, static models are still prevalent throughout the software world. In fact, depending on your definition, they're probably more prevalent than machine learning based AI models. And that's for good reason: manually-tuned models can often outperform machine learning models on a wide variety of tasks. They also have a lower technical barrier for programmers to get their minds around and implement. For many business problems, good old fashioned AI is exactly what you need.

It is also worth noting that static models have found a second life in so-called "hybrid" AI models: complex software that mixes machine learning with static AI. Most autonomous vehicle implementations are a good example of this new paradigm. A static framework for the act of driving (plot a course, look out for obstacles, use the turn signal) provides a useful architecture for specialized machine learning models to then do the algorithmically complex work (e.g., identify specific obstacles).

Machine learning

Machine learning makes up the bulk of the AI technology that has gotten people so excited these past couple of years. As the name implies, machine learning models are ones that "learn": getting better as they are fed more data.

Every machine learning model is made of two major components: the estimation function and the error function. The estimation function does just that: it makes an estimate or prediction about the world. The estimation function is what turns input data into an output. The error function, on the other hand, is what allows the model to learn and become more accurate. Specifically, the error function is a measure of how well the estimation function predicts real world outcomes. Optimization is used to *minimize* the error function by tweaking the parameters of the estimation function. The outcome is the trained model.

The models are not the only interesting type of machine learning technology. There are also several different ways to go about training the models. These are referred to as types of learning.

Types of learning

Supervised

Supervised learning means that a machine learning model is fed input and output data from the real world. It comes to associate the patterns it finds in the input data with given outputs.

Supervised learning constitutes the vast majority of the machine learning that you will come across in a professional context. For the most part, when you hear people talking about applying machine learning to business problems, they are talking specifically about supervised learning.

For instance, you might use supervised learning to create a model that can predict house prices. You might find real estate listings that include factors like square footage and size of yard. You would feed these into the machine learning model along with the output: the prices of the houses. The supervised learning model would learn to associate those input variables with the outcome (the house price).

Unsupervised

As you might surmise, unsupervised learning is a type of model training in which you *don't* give the model output data from the real world. Instead, the unsupervised model seeks to find patterns in the input data and then outputs some kind of information about the patterns that it found.

Unsupervised learning can be helpful in exploring a dataset that you don't know much about. For instance, it can identify the most obvious ways that a dataset can be broken up (i.e., break up a list of property listings based on property type). It can also be used in "hybrid" learning models in which supervised and unsupervised learning are paired, granting the accuracy levels of a supervised learning model without having to invest in a fully tagged dataset.

Unsupervised learning is uncommon for business applications. Most of the time, you will have a good idea of what it is you want to predict and the complexity of implementing a hybrid model outweighs the cost of building a tagged dataset to train a supervised model on.

Reinforcement

Reinforcement learning stands somewhat apart from supervised and unsupervised learning. In fact, you could argue that reinforcement learning models should *also* have the supervised or unsupervised labels applied to them (if you do concern yourself with this, you will run into a second debate on which of the labels applies when).

Reinforcement learning applies to artificially intelligent agents operating in an environment. This may be easiest to visualize in a video game environment. Imagine the game Pong, with a reinforcement learning AI controlling one of the paddles. The agent is allowed any action a human can, namely moving the paddle up or down. The reinforcement agent is also fed a reward function: in this case, the score of the game.

Reinforcement learning is a fascinating area of research for a number of reasons. First, similar to unsupervised learning, it often needs no pre-tagged dataset to begin learning. By operating in its environment, it can create a dataset of its own. Second, it can operate under much more complex conditions than standard supervised or unsupervised models. Third, it is known for having more flexibility in timing between a correct input and a positive outcome (the reward function going up).

If unsupervised learning is rare in a business context, then reinforcement learning may as well not exist. Reinforcement learning is typically much more challenging to implement. The greatest practitioners of reinforcement learning outside of the academic community are DeepMind (AlphaGo) and OpenAI (Dota2 bots), and most of their work is still far from having widespread business uses.

Evolution

I may get some flak from the research community for including evolutionary algorithms as a type of learning. But for the standard non-technical business person, the categorization is useful. You may also hear the term "genetic" algorithm used. Technically genetic algorithms are a type of evolutionary algorithm, but in practice you may think of the two as one in the same.

As you can probably guess, evolutionary algorithms attempt to mimic the natural process of evolution. A model is created and tested. It is then replicated an arbitrary number of times, with randomized "mutations" to key parameters of the model. The best new outcomes are kept, while the worst are removed from the process. There is generally some kind of framework for ensuring that the "traits" of these best performing iterations are passed on to their "offspring".

Evolutionary algorithms have mostly taken a back seat to the other methods of machine learning. They have seen very rare applications in the business world, but for the most part their relevance is confined to an academic setting.

Models

This is a non-exhaustive list of machine learning models. They're organized roughly in terms of complexity, with the simplest at the beginning and the most complicated at the end.

k-nearest neighbors

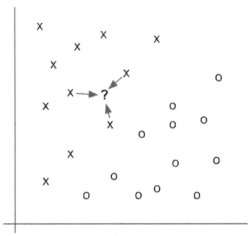

A visualization of the k-nearest neighbors model

k-nearest neighbors is one of the simplest machine learning models. It can be used for either classification or value estimation.

The basic idea of k-nearest neighbors is to take the average value of data points close to the point you're trying to estimate. k represents how many data points you should take the average of.

Say you wanted to predict the value of a house based on its square footage. You have a k-nearest neighbors model with a k value of 2. You're estimating the price of a 2,000 square foot house. Its two closest "neighbors" have square footage of 1,900 and 2,100. To estimate the value of the 2,000 square foot house, you would just average the value of the 1,900 and 2,100 square foot houses.

While k-nearest neighbors is typically trivial to implement, it also typically performs poorly in comparison with other machine learning models that may be able to detect more complicated patterns and take into account non-local information in making predictions.

Linear regression

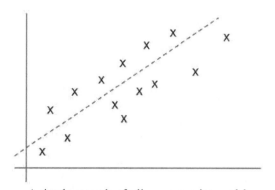

A simple example of a linear regression model

Linear regression is probably the most recognizable machine learning model to non-technical people. Most professionals who have spent much time in a spreadsheet or presentation application have made use of the line fitting functionality on scatter plots. This is an application of linear regression.

Linear regression attempts to fit a line to a set of data points. The line fitting on a scatter plot is the simplest case: a straight line in two dimensions. Linear regression can include an arbitrary number of dimensions and does not need to be a straight line (one common type of curvature is in the sub-class of polynomial regression).

k-means clustering

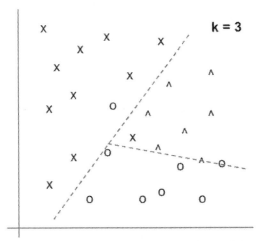

A visualization of the k-means clustering model

k-means clustering is the most common machine learning model that makes use of unsupervised learning. As the name implies, k-means is a type of clustering model: a model that groups data points into related groups. Clustering is differentiated from categorization in that the labels for the clusters are not known (hence unsupervised learning).

Somewhat confusingly, k-means does not bear much resemblance to k-nearest neighbors. The k in each model name actually refers to something entirely different. In k-means, the k represents the total number of clusters that you would like the data broken into. k-means groups the data into the specified number of clusters so as to minimize error.

Clustering may be a bit unintuitive, as you are not explicitly directing the algorithm on how to divide up the dataset. Rather, you direct the algorithm to break the dataset into a number of categories/clusters, and then explore the results to see what you can learn about the natural dividing lines in the data.

You might, for instance, direct a clustering algorithm to break a set of property listings into 3 clusters. Upon investigation, you may find that the clusters loosely affiliate with "house", "apartment", and "waterfront". While that categorization may be strange to a human trying to understand it, there is value in knowing that those three categories best describe the dataset.

Naive Bayes classifier

Naive Bayes classifiers are one of the simplest classification models. They are based on Bayes' Theorem, a formula for determining the probability of a given outcome based on a set of other known outcomes.

Despite their simplicity, naive Bayes classifiers perform remarkably well on many text classification problems. They have been used since the 50s and performed quite well in early email spam detection algorithms. Although more complex (and generally accurate) models are available for text classification, naive Bayes models are often used for their computational efficiency and ease of implementation.

Logistic regression

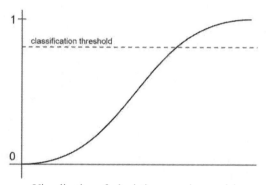

Visualization of a logistic regression model

Although it is a regression model (i.e., numerical estimation), logistic regression is most useful for its classification power. Logistic regression models can be constructed such that their outcomes range from 0 to 1. For classification, a threshold in this range is then established such that any value below the threshold would result in a negative classification (not in the class) and any value above the threshold would be a positive classification (in the class).

Logistic regression models are relatively straightforward to implement and tend to outperform many other basic classifiers like k-nearest neighbor or naive Bayes.

Support vector machine

Similar to k-nearest neighbors, support vector machines (SVMs) can be used for either classification or regression. They are more complex than logistic regression, both conceptually and mathematically. They tend to perform approximately as well as logistic regression on classification problems, though logistic regression has a slight edge overall; SVMs tend to perform better only on certain types of mathematical model constructions.

SVMs work by modeling a boundary between groups of related data points. The model seeks to maximize the total distance between this boundary and each of the points it separates.

In general, the marginal potential improvement in accuracy tends to not justify the complexity of SVMs in practice.

Decision tree

As a reminder, decision trees on their own are actually more a static AI model. They involve a series of comparisons of input variables that can "branch", creating complex "trees" of such comparisons leading to an arbitrary number of outcomes. That being said, decision trees are also commonly used in machine learning.

In the machine learning context, the only difference is that the comparisons that make up the branches of the tree are determined algorithmically so as to maximize the predictive power of the model.

Random forest

Random forests are ensembles of decision trees. In other words, a single random forest is made of a collection of decision tree models acting in concert.

Decision trees are remarkable machine learning models. They are a universal function approximator (meaning they are theoretically capable of modeling any function to an arbitrary level of granularity) and they are generally much easier to parse for humans than other complex machine learning models.

However, decision trees have a tendency to overfit datasets. This isn't a problem unique to decision trees in the machine learning world, but it is a problem that proves challenging to correct in a single decision tree. This is where random forests come in.

A random forest combines a bunch of trained decision trees into a single model to eliminate the overfitting tendency of any of the individual trees. Each decision tree is approximating the same function, but with some randomization thrown in. A type of average is then taken across all of the decision trees. This averaging process corrects for any overfitting that a particular tree may have done.

In practice, random forests are often the most accurate and powerful machine learning model short of a deep neural network. They can be somewhat difficult to implement mathematically, but that difficulty is more or less eliminated by modern machine learning software that takes care of the mechanics for you.

Ensemble

While ensembles are not a type of machine learning model in themselves, it is worth discussing them briefly. As alluded to in the description of random forests, ensembles are collections of machine learning models acting in concert.

Ensembles are useful because certain machine learning models perform particularly well in particular circumstances. For instance, deep neural networks perform particularly well when a large data set is available. However, they perform quite poorly if a data set is sparse. As such, you can imagine an ensemble that uses a deep neural network in data rich environments and a simpler model (e.g., logistic regression) when there is not as much data available.

Markov process

Markov processes are used to model the various states of a system. The model also specifies the patterns of transition among the states for the system.

As opposed to the models explained above, Markov processes are neither estimating a value nor attempting to classify. Instead, they provide information about the likelihood of a system being in a given state at a particular point in time.

In general, Markov processes will not be directly applicable to most business applications. Instead, they are used as a behind-the-scenes technology for interim applications, such as natural language processing and voice-to-text.

Markov processes, while not necessarily more complex than the other machine learning models, are generally less used by the broad machine learning community. As such, when they are applied to relevant problems, such as what DeepMind did with its reinforcement learning, they can result in relatively unique and powerful models with a high barrier to replication.

Gaussian process

Gaussian processes are an advanced form of regression that can be useful when a simple prediction of a value is not sufficient. Whereas normal regression models provide a single value for any given input (i.e., a 2,000 square foot house is predicted to cost $300,000), Gaussian models provide a *distribution* of values.

This additional information and complexity can be useful in applications where it is important to know the accuracy, uncertainty, or distribution of an estimate. For instance, a prediction that the stock market will go up by 100 points tomorrow may not be as useful as knowing the distribution of possible outcomes, including that there is a 25% chance that it goes *down* by more than 100 points.

Gaussian processes are relatively uncommon in industry. They are more difficult to model (requiring more expertise from your data scientists) and require much more computation time than more simple regression models.

Artificial neural network

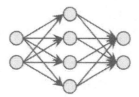

A basic neural network

Artificial neural networks (ANNs) are exactly what they sound like: mathematical models meant to replicate the problem solving ability of the neural networks in the human brain. While many AI practitioners will rail against this characterization of these models due to concerns about hype, they cannot escape the fact that this was the motivation for the development of ANNs, starting with the artificial neuron invented by McCulloch and Pitts in 1943.

ANNs are typically modeled using a graph diagram, where each node represents a "neuron" in the network and each edge represents a "synapse" connecting two neurons. The basic ANN has a neuron for each input, a neuron for each output, and a "layer" of "hidden" neurons for signal transformation in between. This transformation can take different forms, but one of the most common is that each neuron essentially functions as a distinct logistic regression model–meaning ANNs may be much more complex than simpler machine learning models.

Deep neural network

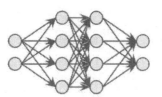

A basic deep neural network

Deep neural networks (DNNs) are a particular class of neural network. In fact, they are the only type of neural network that is really relevant today. The only difference between a DNN and a basic ANN is that a DNN has more than one hidden layer. In other words, the signal from the inputs goes through more than one layer of transformation before reaching the output layer. The number of hidden layers varies widely based on the specific model (ranging from two to thousands).

As a reminder, DNNs are the underlying technology behind most of the modern advances in AI that have driven the excitement in the field.

DNNs are particularly well-suited to processing massive amounts of unstructured information that have defied more traditional methods of data processing. These types of data include images, video, sound, and text documents.

While all machine learning models require sizable sets of data to train up to a high level of accuracy, DNNs have particularly large data requirements. While a basic naive Bayes classifier may achieve 90%+ levels of accuracy on some problems with hundreds of training data points, a DNN may need tens or hundreds of thousands.

Recurrent neural network

Recurrent neural networks (RNNs) are a particular sub-class of DNNs. RNNs are most commonly applied to datasets that are meant to be processed locally (as opposed to globally). Most often, this means audio or text. The RNN will digest a chunk of the overall dataset, process it, commit an impression of it to "memory" and then move on to the next chunk. Each subsequent processing step utilizes the information that came before it. This is conceptually similar to how a human digests such information: converting the raw signal (e.g., noise/vibrations) into meaning (e.g., words, concepts) progressively.

Specifically, you may come across a type of RNN called long short-term memory (LSTM), which refers to a specific mechanism for storing and using the "memory". In practice, almost all relevant RNNs are LSTMs and you can treat the two terms as synonyms.

Convolutional neural network

Convolutional neural networks (CNNs or ConvNets) are another sub-class of DNNs. As described in the "History of AI" chapter, CNNs were inspired by a neurobiological understanding of the visual cortex of animals.

The "convolution" part of CNNs is essentially a series of processing steps applied to a dataset before it is fed into the DNN. These convolutions are looking for "features" in the data. One intuitive type of convolution in image processing is edge detection: picking out sharp transitions between colors. In practice, these convolutions may be more abstract and may not have any intuitive meaning to a human observer.

The idea behind CNNs is that before you have the DNN take a crack at analyzing data, you first try to find higher-level patterns. You then feed those *patterns* into the DNN, as opposed to the raw data. This is how the visual cortex works for humans. The neurons close to the eye are picking out features of what you see before handing the signal off to the brain; the brain as a whole actually never gets the raw data.

CNNs are particularly adept at image processing. They first rose to prominence in the 1980s for their accuracy at optical character recognition (OCR), more colloquially known as hand-writing recognition. CNNs were behind the "conquering" of the ImageNet competition in 2015, in which they showed their use in accurately identifying objects in digital images. In the past couple of years, researchers have begun to apply CNNs to more and more types of information with increasing success. There is some evidence to suggest they may be able to supplant RNNs as the dominant model for text and audio processing as well.

Generative adversarial network

An example of a GAN-generated image, taken from thispersondoesnotexist.com

Generative adversarial networks (GANs) are another sub-class of DNNs. Technically, they are actually a combination of two distinct DNNs working together.

Up until now, this book has mostly talked about AI as it pertains to information processing: taking in data about the world and coming up with some sort of insight. There is actually an entire domain of AI dedicated to the opposite problem: how to *generate* data. However, historically, these models have substantially lagged their processing brethren.

GANs represent a step-change improvement in the use of AI models for creation. The basic idea is this: two DNNs are strapped together. The first DNN is tasked with creating some type of content (let's say an image). The second DNN is then tasked with determining whether that image is real or fake: whether it is human-generated or machine-generated. To keep things fair, the second DNN is intermittently fed real images so it can't just always guess "fake".

GANs were a direct reaction to the major weakness of more traditional generative models. Most generative AI models are *capable* of creating high quality content, but cannot do so *reliably*. They might generate 99 low quality images for each one that looks like the real thing. Astute researchers decided that rather than using their own precious human time to pick out the

1 from the 99, *they would train an AI system to do so*. And to do that, Ian Goodfellow first proposed the GAN in 2014.

Of all the technologies discussed in this book, GANs likely have the most medium-term potential for massive impact. In a world fraught with concern over "fake news", imagine if high quality video could *actually* be created for virtually no cost artificially, on-demand. GANs are already doing this today, with high profile "DeepFakes" affecting celebrities and politicians.

Chapter 5

Applications of AI

Applications of artificial intelligence sit in between technologies and use cases: they're not code-level implementations of intelligence, but also not quite commercial-ready business solutions as most people would recognize them.

Applications of AI typically make use of one or more technologies to achieve a slightly higher-level outcome. In many cases, the underlying technologies can be treated as exchangeable building blocks with slightly different performance, but essentially the same purpose.

Similarly: on their own, AI applications are typically not sufficient to solve meaningful real-world problems (with a few notable exceptions, like anomaly detection). They may have to be combined with one another or packaged into a broader process or set of software tools. The sophistication of any given application can vary widely; you may need to package a handful of basic applications together before achieving the level of apparent intelligence that a single more advanced application might achieve.

Although business professionals will most commonly be working more directly with the use cases of artificial intelligence, it is very important to understand the applications that underlie them. A solid understanding at this level will help you understand what is possible and how different implementations of the technologies might best fit together.

Structured Data

From a machine learning standpoint, it is generally much easier to work with structured data versus unstructured. In many cases, this is true for other types of AI as well. Structured data (i.e., well-organized numerical data) is much easier for computers to parse. Unstructured data (text, images, audio), on the other hand, is far less easy to handle for most systems.

As such, many of the early applications of AI were concerned mostly with structured data. As the tools of the field were being developed, it was too much to ask the practitioners to also figure out how to wrangle arbitrary data into a structure programmatically. AI applications tailored to structured data are some of the oldest and most well-understood in the field.

Categorization

"Classification" was discussed in the AI Technologies chapter of this book. In most cases, classification models are performing some kind of "categorization" application. In other words, they take a set of input data and break them into categories or some kind of organizational structure.

At its most basic, categorization can take numerical data and categorize it. Google's Nest thermostat, for instance, might categorize different temperature settings as "user at home" or "user away". These types of applications are ubiquitous in the commercial world, but typically take a substantial amount of additional packaging to form meaningful use cases.

Categorization of non-numerical data may be more recognizable to the average consumer. AI-driven categorization has shown up across such varied domains as movies, articles, books, and songs. However, because these applications are analyzing unstructured media, they rely on intermediary algorithms (which may or may not qualify as AI in their own right) to transform the data into a structured input for the categorization application itself.

Recommendation system

Recommendation systems were one of the most prolific AI implementations for consumer use cases at the forefront of the current AI wave. Two of the most prominent were created by Amazon and Netflix to make product and movie recommendations, respectively.

A recommendation system seeks to predict how a user would score a given entity based on knowledge of past scorings. A common scale for recommendation systems relies on 1-5 stars. These predictions can be made across a body of potential entities, then the top set of entities is fed to the user as actual recommendations.

Recommendation systems can also be implemented as categorizers. Instead of coming up with a predicted score, they can instead predict a binary classification: interesting to the user or not. They can be made to reduce the number of recommendations by increasing the threshold for an outcome to be predicted as "interesting".

As with categorization, recommendation systems often rely on intermediary technology to convert unstructured data into structured.

Anomaly detection

Anomaly detection attempts to identify data points that stand out as abnormal from a data set. One basic implementation of anomaly detection is the concept of outliers from statistics. More advanced implementations might attempt to detect more complex patterns in the data, rather than mapping it all out on a single distribution.

In some contexts, anomaly detection can also be considered a use case on its own. This is particularly prevalent in the industrial world for predictive maintenance use cases. An anomaly detection system might look for aberrant measurements from a suite of sensors and flag the anomaly to a supervisor in order to prevent some kind of expensive failure.

However, anomaly detection is also used in a variety of other domains as part of a broader intelligent solution. For instance, anomaly detection might be used to detect a fraudulent transaction attempt by a website or identify a customer service agent going off-script in their customer interactions.

Natural Language

One of the largest areas of artificial intelligence application is concerned with natural language. In this context, natural language is meant as a distinction from machine language (binary, or some abstraction of it). In other words, natural language is language that humans understand and use to communicate. For the American audience, this is typically spoken or written English.

There are a variety of different ways that AI can interact with language to perform tasks that have historically been the exclusive domain of humans. Although there are many use cases that these applications tie to, at their root natural language AI applications are largely focused on making the power of computers available in more convenient ways to a larger audience. When people talk about the average person being able to "program" a computer by teaching it, they are in no small part referring to the ability for someone to interface with the computer in a way which has historically been limited to those who knew programming languages.

Natural Language Processing (NLP)

Just as it sounds, Natural Language Processing (NLP) is the use of AI to turn language into some other kind of—often enriched—information. NLP is one of the single most common applications of AI. And for good reason: language is the tool of communication for humans. As computers become more integrated into the majority of our information flow, their ability to work with the way we communicate becomes ever more important.

While NLP is trending toward using more advanced technologies, historical NLP applications have relied on remarkably simple (from an AI perspective) technologies. Much of the non-machine learning work in the field of AI over the course of the decades leading to the current surge in AI interest resulted in NLP applications.

Under the broad NLP umbrella, there are a wide array of smaller applications that can either be used on their own for very basic processing tasks or—more commonly—combined to tackle a more difficult problem. Each of these tasks may make use of one or more AI technologies, with ranging levels of sophistication. Some are so basic as to be difficult to classify as AI on their own, similar to the linear regression application in your spreadsheet software.

Stemming

Stemming (also called "lemmatization") is one of the most basic sub-applications within NLP. Quite simply, it involves taking a body of words and stripping each word down to its "stem". In its simplest form, a stemming algorithm would take words like "eats" and "eating" and identify that the root word is "eat".

Many applications of stemming rely on basic rules: a defined set of translations from words to their roots. This approach is simple, quick, and effective for many languages (including English). It does fall short for some other languages and also cannot cope with words that it has not been explicitly programmed for ("tweetstorms" for instance). In these cases, more advanced methods may rely on stochastic analysis or pre-processing like part-of-speech tagging.

Stemming is useful in basic applications of AI and when there is relatively little training data. In these cases, assuming all words that share a root are heavily related can help get results quickly. For more advanced NLP applications, however, stemming may cause the algorithm to ignore important information about words (i.e., *how* they have changed from the root word, and what that means for the sentence's meaning).

Tokenizing

Tokenizing is the process of breaking language down into smaller chunks for discrete analysis. Virtually no algorithms can process an arbitrary-length body of text in a single go: they must first break the text down into its components. This is how human language processing works as well; for example, you cannot absorb the entirety of this book from one look at all of its words laid out in front of you.

The most common length of a token in NLP is a word. This is a common unit for basic applications of stemming, part-of-speech tagging, and several other types of NLP. However, tokens are often larger and may even be smaller.

While considering language word by word may be the easiest approach, much of the meaning in language is based on the interconnection of words. As such, multi-word or sentence-length tokens are necessary for any NLP beyond the basics. Multi-word tokens are often referred to as n-grams, where n represents the number of words (e.g., unigram, bigram, etc.).

In some cases, analyzing text at the sub-word level may be helpful. For instance, separating a word into its stem and its prefixes and suffixes may help understand how that word is being used in context.

Part-of-speech tagging

As you might guess, part-of-speech tagging is taking in a body of words and identifying the part-of-speech (e.g., noun, verb) for each. While simple on its surface, this is a surprisingly difficult—and important—problem at the root of advanced NLP applications.

Basic part-of-speech tagging algorithms will rely on a dictionary of word / part-of-speech pairs, with some kind of stochastic analysis for determining the part-of-speech when there are multiple possibilities.

One modest complexity comes from the number of parts of speech: while the average professional could come up with a handful relatively easily, they may not realize how many there actually are. While there is not a unified group of tags for parts-of-speech, one of the more commonly used tagging models in English makes use of 36.

Still, to a program 36 categorizations is not algorithmically much more complex than a handful. The real challenge comes in the ambiguity that is prolific throughout almost all human communications. Any given word may have the possibility of being a variety of different parts of speech, depending on the context that the word is used in.

While disambiguation is natural and mostly effortless for humans, it's an incredibly complex problem for computers. Highly accurate part-of-speech tagging relies on accurate disambiguation, which is discussed more in the "syntax parsing" section in a few pages.

Part-of-speech tagging is critical for many NLP applications to get beyond a surface analysis of language. Most applications that rely on understanding the interaction between words in a sentence will depend on knowing the part-of-speech in each word. As such, part-of-speech tagging and syntax parsing are very interconnected, as opposed to being distinct linear steps in processing.

Embedding

Cat

animal	1.0
object	0.3
friendly	-0.2
wet	-0.5
food	-0.5
quadruped	0.8
vertebrate	0.9

A simple example of a word embedding

Embedding wins the award for (arguably) being the least intuitive of the NLP applications discussed here.

Word embedding involves converting words into numerical vectors. Technically, many forms of AI-based language analysis such as classification and sentiment analysis also do this. Those applications, in their basic forms, use a dimension in vector space for every single unique word from a body of language; the vectors might then have occurrences or frequencies of each word stored in them.

Embedding simplifies these massive dimensionality vectors into smaller ones representing more abstract concepts. These more abstract dimensions can be designed intentionally—in such a way that they have meaning within the context of an application—or programmatically so as to maximize a desirable outcome.

Embedding is most often used as a preprocessing step for some further NLP application such as syntax parsing or sentiment analysis, and has been shown to greatly improve results in some cases. The most well-known implementation of word embedding is Google's Word2Vec.

Topic identification

Topic identification is just that: recognizing the primary topic or set of topics from a body of text. Topic identification is often an important stepping stone toward more complex NLP applications that perform some further analysis or action based on what a block of language is referring to.

In some ways, topic identification is an extension of part-of-speech tagging: all—or at least most—nouns in a set of text are topics of some form or fashion. The key to most applications of topic identification is to cut out the noise of all these nouns to focus in on the ones that particularly matter for a given context.

Topic identification is the first NLP application that begins to resemble what many would identify as a use case of AI. Through the 1990s and 2000s, a large number of software tools were developed to perform topic identification (and often sentiment analysis, which will be covered shortly) on large bodies of text. These were most often applied in a voice of the customer context—for instance on survey responses—to draw insights out of a large number of perspectives without time intensive human review.

Topic identification is often a critical first step in the more advanced NLP application of text summarization (which will be covered shortly). The idea is that if you can identify the important topics of a block of language, then you can build out the context and why they are important.

Named entity recognition (NER)

Named entity recognition (NER) shares similarities with part-of-speech tagging and topic identification. The purpose of NER is to identify "named" things: people, places, essentially proper nouns.

While this is an easy enough task for well-recognized names like David and when you can expect proper capitalization, the task gets fairly tricky for more generic cases:

catching names that you may not know ahead of time and not being able to rely on capitalization.

NER is important because it is often necessary for accurate topic identification, particularly given how central many named entities are in arbitrary passages of text.

Syntax parsing

Syntax parsing is used to understand the roles and interrelationships of each word in a sentence. It relies on part-of-speech tagging, but also models out how each of the words—and the phrases they are a part of—fits into the sentence as a whole.

Syntax parsing is at the root of machines (and humans!) understanding natural language. Take, for instance, the sentence "I drove to eat my food, which was good." Most humans have no issue assuming the food in the sentence was good. But it is also perfectly valid to assume that the overall experience was good or that driving (versus walking, for instance) was good. It all depends which word the phrase "which was good" is modifying. Humans figure this out very quickly and relatively easily. Computers have a much harder time.

Basic syntax parsing is based on statistical rules. A set of data with defined relationships is fed into a model. The frequency of given applications of the syntax rules is then used to parse new sentences. The problem is that these systems are unwieldy, hard to update, and not very flexible; particularly for complex sentences.

Human-level syntax parsing is commonly considered to be an AI-Hard problem, meaning that it requires human-level general AI. This is because highly accurate parsing implies understanding the meaning of a sentence. True understanding of language meaning is widely believed to be a marker of AGI.

Sentiment analysis

Sentiment analysis is a common application of AI on natural language. It involves determining the overall sentiment of a block of text. For instance, "happy" has a positive sentiment and "sad" has a negative sentiment. Sentiment analysis can be used to determine the sentiment of an entire document or of distinct portions (i.e., a sentence at a time).

Basic sentiment analysis depends on a simple pre-determined sentiment score defined for each word, similar to the "happy" and "sad" example from the previous paragraph. While this approach is fairly effective for very basic applications, it has many points of failure. It might, for instance, interpret "not very happy" as a positive sentiment. This can be corrected using n-grams of greater length than one word, though the problem of defining a sentiment score for every combination of every word quickly becomes intractable. Another quick solution involves applying basic rules (e.g., treating "not" as a negator).

More advanced sentiment analysis may attempt to make use of more sophisticated syntax parsing to better understand the structure of a sentence and interpret sentiment on a context-specific basis.

It is worth briefly noting that sentiment analysis is just one example of a broad class of natural language applications that assess a block of text's value against a dimension. For instance, using similar concepts from sentiment analysis, you could train a model to determine how professional a memo is or how urgent an email is.

Text summarization

Text summarization is fairly intuitive: an application of AI to take in a body of text and generate an accurate summary. Where topic identification can pull out the most important or relevant nouns, summarization builds on that functionality by putting these topics into a broader context.

As with syntax parsing, human-level text summarization is considered to be an AI-Hard problem: any AI application that could summarize text as well as a human would have to be generally as intelligent as a human.

With that in mind, you may find that there is a significant amount of misleading advertising around text summarization solutions available on the market as of 2019. Companies are already marketing solutions that they claim can generate summaries of calls and meetings at human- or near-human-levels of accuracy. These claims are not true: while there are functional text summarization solutions available today, they do not truly achieve results comparable to most humans.

Basic text summarization today will often use relatively basic rules to extract particular fragments from a longer body of text. For instance, a solution might summarize the average news article by pulling out the first sentence, a random sentence from the first major header, and then a sentence from the last paragraph of the article. Taken together, these sentences could be seen as a decent summarization of some articles. But these rules are inflexible and clearly miss a lot of potentially valuable information throughout the rest of the article.

Even more sophisticated solutions for text summarization are still often based on relatively basic rules. They might, for instance, use a relatively basic classifier to identify sentences that are more likely to be important. But they are still just reporting select sentences. These relatively basic methods are known as extraction-based: they extract text they believe to accurately reflect the message of the overall document.

A truly accurate text summarization solution will ultimately need to take what is known as an abstraction-based approach: understanding the meaning of the document and then repackaging it. This is how human text summarization works. There are virtually no text summarization solutions on the market today that attempt to understand the true meaning of a large body of text.

The difficulty of abstraction-based methodologies—and the accompanying improvement in summarization accuracy—is two-fold. Beyond the need for more accurate understanding of the content of a document, abstraction methods must then store that knowledge in some information format and *then* create a summary from scratch based on that knowledge. This last step is a Natural Language Generation (NLG) problem; despite the similarity in name, NLG is a distinct application from NLP and is considered to be substantially more difficult.

Natural Language Understanding (NLU)

Natural Language Understanding (NLU) is a lesser-used term to describe some particularly sophisticated NLP applications. There is no formal distinction between NLP and NLU; in fact, a substantial amount of the usage of the term "NLU" is being driven by companies seeking to differentiate their relatively ordinary NLP software through marketing. As such, any references to NLU in a commercial context should be considered with a fair degree of skepticism.

In theory, NLU is defined separately from NLP so as to exclude some of the more basic applications mentioned in the previous section. A statistical approach to part-of-speech tagging or sentiment analysis, for instance, would not generally be considered sophisticated enough to connote "understanding" in the way that humans think about language.

The applications where NLU are most relevant are the ones where a human-like understanding of language is necessary for accuracy or effectiveness. As mentioned in the previous section, these applications include highly accurate part-of-speech tagging, syntax parsing, and text summarization.

In informal usage, some use the term NLU to refer to a human level of understanding of language. As previously mentioned, this implies AGI: human-level artificial general intelligence. In practice, this term is somewhat redundant: people saying "no true NLU exists" are essentially saying the same thing as "no AGI exists", which is not particularly useful or disputed information.

Much of the current focus on NLU advancement as it pertains to use cases is perhaps better categorized as Natural Language Querying (NLQ), which will be covered more thoroughly shortly. One of the most visible failures of language understanding today is the difficulty computers have in interpreting human commands in natural language (like Siri). Outside of NLQ, much of the bottleneck on human-level AI development rests more squarely in knowledge representation and abstract problem solving than natural language specifically.

Natural Language Generation (NLG)

As you might expect from its name, the application of Natural Language Generation (NLG) involves using AI to create language (specifically in text format). While—on its surface—

this might seem like much the same thing as NLP (just in reverse), the reality is that NLG is considered to be a *much* more difficult application of AI and has significantly fewer systems implementing it, whether commercial or academic.

Single word generation

Just as with NLP, NLG can tackle varying lengths of language at a given time. The applications that have seen the most success in the real world—and have therefore seen the most implementations—are largely concerned with using NLG on a single word at a time.

While there are a number of different experimental use cases for single world NLG, it is fairly closely associated with one particular successful use case: autocorrect and auto-suggest, mostly now used on smartphones.

Basic single word NLG applications rely on a straightforward set of rules. In the autocorrect example, this would be a predefined table of common misspellings and their correct associations. In past decades, these applications have gotten progressively more sophisticated: evolving from static rules to statistical rules to more advanced methods that depend on more sophisticated NLP on surrounding context.

Document generation

Similar to text summarization in NLP, NLG can be applied to entire bodies of text or documents at once. In this case, an algorithm might write a news story or even an entire novel without any input from a human.

Despite being more interesting and getting more attention from casual AI observers, the use of AI for document generation is still an incredibly nascent application. Although there are systems that can create syntactically correct sentences, doing so in a way that communicates valuable meaning has proven to be a remarkably difficult problem. Stringing *multiple* such sentences together—much less paragraphs, pages, or chapters— is a virtual impossibility with today's technology.

That being said, there are a handful of solutions in the market today that make claims around document generation using AI. These providers are not (typically) *lying*, but their claims can be misleading if you don't understand the underlying solutions they are implementing.

The most common approach of solutions claiming to use AI to generate documents is to create the documents according to predefined templates and sets of rules. There are a number of relatively small companies using this methodology to generate news articles, primarily around financial reporting and sports. These domains have a component of reporting that is highly formulaic: "company X saw a 10% increase in stock price after announcing quarterly earnings 3% above expectations". In these cases, a solution that amounts to "fill in the blank" can get the job done. While the documents generated by such solutions will not make for engaging journalism, they may fill a real need.

There are some limited examples of claims of AI systems creating more creative and free-form documents. These examples include poems, songs, novels, and screenplays. While there is no unifying "gotcha" across these examples, it is safe to say that there is always more than meets the eye. One of the more common methods involves using AI in a series of well-defined subtasks and stitching together the results. For instance, using an algorithm to generate character and location names, as well as a basic (and formulaic) plot line, that is then "filled in" by a human writer. Another is to use a true generative model to come up with hundreds or thousands of documents, then selecting the best among them (the other 99.9% may be very low quality).

Natural Language Querying (NLQ)

Natural Language Querying (NLQ) is the combination of NLP and NLG to allow back-and-forth interaction between a human and a computer. This is the AI application that empowers the digital assistant use case, like Siri or Alexa.

While NLQ is not necessarily a distinct application from NLP or NLG, the interplay between the two creates some unique challenges and there are some specific problems in each domain that are particularly relevant to the NLQ application.

Similar to text summarization from the NLP section, high quality NLQ typically relies on some form of abstraction. It is not typically sufficient for an advanced NLQ system to have prepared responses to queries that are known ahead of time. That does not mean that this approach is not used; it's just limited to basic implementations. These NLQ applications may end up looking more similar to a command line interface than an AI agent, where human input must take a very structured form and the computer output is nearly always templatized.

The necessity of abstraction for an advanced NLQ system makes most NLQ applications more challenging than standard NLP applications. This challenge is magnified by the type of task the application is performing: people consider query/response behavior to be more human-like than some basic text processing, and therefore attach higher expectations to NLQ applications.

It is worth further exploring some of the challenges and applications within NLQ.

Intent recognition

With the framing that NLQ is primarily concerned with scenarios in which queries are generated by the human, one of the biggest tasks for the NLQ application is to determine the intent of the input query. In the simple command line-like version, this is quite straightforward: the system recognizes a well-defined set of inputs. A basic extension of that application could use an ontology or set of synonyms to provide some flexibility in recognizing the input.

However, for anything beyond a basic system, an NLQ application must have fairly sophisticated intent recognition. The variability with which a person might communicate any given intent is orders of magnitude more complicated than it might seem at first glance. To manage this complexity, many NLQ applications will heavily restrict the domain that they operate in. While determining intent for even a single type of command or query can be challenging, it becomes more so extralinearly as the number of supported queries increases.

Sophisticated intent recognition will often begin by determining the type of query: question, command, etc. For questions, the application will then attempt to determine which domain of its knowledge the question is attempting to access (or whether it has the requisite knowledge at all). Similarly, for commands, the application will attempt to determine which supported command, if any, the user is attempting to interact with.

Once the domain of the query is determined, sophisticated systems will then attempt to customize its response or action according to details provided by the user in the query. While determining domain is difficult, getting the details right for arbitrary cases is currently an unsolved problem, and is likely an AI-Hard problem requiring human-level AGI.

Question answering

The outcome of intent recognition can take many different forms but one of the most common is a request to answer a question. Once the question has been determined, the system must be able to query against some form of knowledge base to provide an answer (assuming the answer resides in the knowledge base).

This type of question answering application is a relatively well-studied problem on its own. In fact, in many circumstances this is considered to be a solved problem. IBM's Watson solved the problem for the game show format Jeopardy back in 2011. In January of 2018 it was announced that the problem had been solved for generic questions about Wikipedia articles (according to the SQuAD dataset).

To be clear, question answering is only a solved problem for well-defined questions that have answers stored in a knowledge set. Determining the meaning of less-well-defined questions is the domain of intent recognition and more complicated question answering may require some form of abstraction, which is still very much unsolved.

Disaggregation

While advanced intent recognition is still very much an unsolved problem, there is already a need to think beyond it. Most NLQ applications have an implicit assumption that there is one domain, action, or question for each user query. However, in practice, people often formulate more complex queries that may require more than one action or answer.

Very advanced NLQ applications attempt to address this challenge by not making assumptions about the number of underlying intents per query. Instead, they attempt to identify individual intents, however many there may be. This type of intent disaggregation is incredibly challenging from a technical perspective and often relies on high quality syntax parsing.

The problem of query disaggregation is challenging enough that most solution providers in the space have opted to shape user behavior to ensure a single intent per query instead of attempting to solve the problem. However, the problem is getting more attention in recent years due to the rise of digital assistants.

Context tracking

Another significant extension of basic intent recognition is an NLQ application's ability to keep track of context over the course of a conversation. The vast majority of systems today are only capable of working with a single query at a time: user provides query, machine provides response or action. Again, this does not mirror how people expect a query agent to operate. Human conversations have many back-and-forth interactions and each participant is expected to remember the thread of the conversation over the course of multiple queries.

More advanced NLQ applications may attempt to take the context of the earlier conversation into account as they attempt to understand a user's intent in the most recent query. By doing so, they enable users to use pronouns and shorter queries, which feels far more natural. As mentioned previously, computers have far more difficult dealing with ambiguity in language than humans do. These cross-query context tracking tasks introduce a great amount of ambiguity.

Machine Translation

Machine translation makes use of AI to translate from one language to another (e.g., Spanish to English). Machine translation is a somewhat odd application in that it is—for the most part—a use case as well: AI translation of languages is also recognized by most people as a value-generating task on its own.

Machine translation has seen significant progress in the past few years. Until 2015 or so, most machine translation systems still relied on phrase-based rules that would generally convey the idea of a sentence, but often had awkward and confusing wording or vocabulary. This approach was similar to other basic NLP approaches: understand the rules of language, the context in which the translation might be happening, and either set out static rules or relatively basic statistical ones.

This traditional approach to machine translation has been almost entirely replaced by a deep learning approach. In the span of just a year or two, AI machine translation went from limited application to near-human-level and integrated into many popular technologies (like Facebook and Twitter).

The basic application of deep learning to machine translation is focused on direct translation from one language to another. On their own, these models can perform quite well. The drawback is that a separate model must be trained for each combination of languages. While not an intractable problem, it can be costly to build up datasets and train that many models.

More recent and advanced applications of deep learning to machine translation make use of a type of abstraction: they use a sort of intermediary language or knowledge representation system, which allows for substantially more flexibility between arbitrary languages. This intermediary step is not generally interpretable by humans. This has led to some widely distributed headlines about machines inventing their own language that humans don't understand. While true in some ways, it is worth noting that this is how the applications were programmed to work, and there is still no agency on the AI's part.

Rich Media

Traditional AI approaches have mostly been limited to structured data and text processing. In a world where AI was dominated by manual application of rules and statistics, this made sense: the amount of data that exists in media like images and sound is generally too large to be easily manageable by a human's manual efforts.

While the potential for deep learning to work with rich media has been explored for decades, it is only recently that the hardware has advanced to the point that the deep learning models can run at a reasonable speed. Now that the potential has been demonstrated clearly, exploration of the use of AI on rich media has taken off rapidly, with significant advances in the past few years.

Visual media

Optical Character Recognition (OCR)

One of the earliest commercial applications of AI on visual media was called Optical Character Recognition (OCR). OCR is actually one of the first clearly demonstrated applications of deep learning to a real world problem.

OCR involves using AI to process text out of an unstructured data format (i.e., a photo). OCR systems almost always break the text down into its component characters for individual processing.

OCR has essentially been a solved problem with superhuman performance for years, and is fairly prolific in various commercial use cases like mail sorting and document digitization.

Object recognition

As OCR is to text, object recognition is to generic things. Historically this was an intractable problem for AI, detecting specific three dimensional objects with their variations in orientation, coloring, shadowing, and shapes was a far more difficult problem than simple text.

There were major breakthroughs in object recognition around 2014, as it became more practical to apply convolutional neural networks to larger images. Today, object recognition is a solved problem with superhuman performance in many contexts. That being said, the analysis required for object recognition is still heavily hardware dependent and is limited in its ability to process large images quickly.

Computer vision

Computer vision is the use of AI to process information about the world through a visual input (i.e., photo or video). OCR and object recognition are both sub-applications under the broader umbrella of computer vision.

Other than OCR, much of the early advancement of computer vision was driven by the robotics use case: computer agents attempting to physically navigate and manipulate the real world. The major commercial incentive for this advancement came from industrial robots: typically some kind of manipulator performing an action on a physical good. Given this context, early computer vision became quite good at being able to detect small differences in a very confined setting (e.g., slight mis-rotation of a product on an assembly line).

The proliferation of deep learning (and particularly convolutional neural networks) applied to computer vision has allowed for increasing abstraction of the types of information that AI systems can pull out of visual inputs. Beyond object recognition, these more modern systems are able to parse out *multiple* objects from the same image, understand the actions they may be taking, and interpret the broader context of a given image.

Video analysis is an interesting application. Today, most systems analyzing video are actually analyzing individual frames of video as images and then placing those individual frame analyses in some kind of broader context. These applications are typically sampling frames instead of processing all of the information available.

However, there are some early efforts to process video data more holistically: carrying over context from one frame to the next inherently in the model, similar to how recurrent neural networks have a memory for the data they have processed.

Image/video generation

As with all types of AI, generative models have always substantially lagged processing models. This is perhaps doubly true for visual media historically.

There have been some limited attempts to create digital images using AI in past decades. These have mostly been constrained to the artistic realm, and in more abstract styles there. There are a couple of instances of systems creating fairly unique works, but they are relatively few and far between and nearly always have human intervention.

The past couple of years have seen more advancement in this application than the rest of AI's history combined. Nearly all of this progress can be attributed to Generative Adversarial Networks (GANs) and Variational Autoencoders (VAEs). These models, developed recently, overcome one of the major flaws of older generative AI models: the vast majority of their output is not recognizable to humans. GANs have vastly improved the accuracy of generative models, particularly in the realm of image and video generation.

Image generation applications are still mostly academic, just given how nascent the use of GANs and VAEs is. However, that is changing rapidly as the commercial potential of the technology is explored.

Some early applications of GANs to images include raw generation (e.g., you tell the system to draw a bird and it does so with no further input), style transfer (adapting the artistic style of one image to another), and image manipulation (e.g., changing a picture of a frowning face to a smiling face). The technology has also been turned to video and has created convincing samples of manipulating a person's lip movements arbitrarily (so as to mimic speech of any kind).

Audio media

Of the various sources of unstructured data, audio has tended to get the least attention from the AI field. This is partly because one of audio's most important abilities as information is to communicate language, which is generally better represented as text than audio for most applications. Still, there are several applications of AI to audio data that have meaningful commercial adoption and significant potential.

Voice-to-text

The most common application of AI to audio media is to convert spoken language into text. This is what drives much of the intelligence of solutions like Siri and Alexa.

Since late 2017, numerous technology companies have claimed to have solved this problem, at least in constrained environments (i.e., conversational quality with a single speaker). Indeed, most consumers have noticed the drastic improvements in voice-to-text quality since the first mass-consumer application of Siri in 2011. While transcription errors are still common and form the butt of many jokes, more and more people are coming to rely on voice-to-text applications for their interface with computers.

Voice-to-text is at the core of what some are predicting as a mass transformation of human-computer interface. Where historical interface was primarily keyboard and mouse driven, many predict that as voice-to-text technology progresses, many (most?) interface will transition to voice-based. While the most aggressive timelines for this transformation have already been shown to be unrealistic, there is new interest in the paradigm as voice-to-text applications pass the human-level accuracy threshold.

There is substantial opportunity for voice-to-text to transform audio transcription. Currently, the transcription market is relatively modest; mostly due to the prohibitive expense of having humans manually transcribe recordings. As voice-to-text reaches superhuman capabilities in the commercial sphere, the cost of transcription is likely to drop by at least an order of magnitude, opening significant opportunity for disruption. In that near-future, transcription may become a reality for many more uses (e.g., recording and transcribing every business meeting or conference call).

Between human-computer interface and transcription, voice-to-text is one of the AI applications with the most potential for disruption in the near future.

Sound recognition

Sound recognition is the general application of AI to analyze audio data. While voice-to-text is a particular sub-application within the sound recognition umbrella, there are some applications of sound recognition outside of the voice domain.

AI models can be trained to accurately identify a wide variety of sounds: loud noises, particular bird calls, etc. These problems are relatively solved. However, they have not received much attention (in a relative sense) from either the academic or commercial communities. So far, their real-world uses have not been all that apparent.

One prominent example of a sound recognition application is for song recognition, as popularized by the Shazam app. Song recognition will typically extract some kind of signature from a song (i.e., beat, cadence, levels, etc.) and match it to a known database of song signatures.

Another relatively small exception to the general lack of interest in sound recognition has been the recent use of AI to identify gunshots in high-crime urban areas. Systems have been implemented to identify the sound of a gun firing and immediately notify law enforcement of the event and its approximate location.

Audio generation

Just as with the other forms of media, AI can be used to generate audio as well as process it. There have been some limited tests of AI to generate music, animal sounds, and various other ambient noises. However, the domain that has received by far the most attention has been voice generation.

Traditional voice generation models (like Siri) have relied on a manual collection of recorded syllables or sounds. These individual pieces are then stitched together to form words and sentences. This stitching process is what has historically led to the "robotic" sound of generated voices.

In the past year or so, voice generation has progressed rapidly. For the first time, in December 2017, it was announced that a model had been developed to generate near-professional-human-level voice recordings. In the year or two since, high profile commercial use cases like Google's Duplex have moved voice generation close to the category of "solved" problems.

One interesting facet of the recent advances in voice generation is that many of the models are capable of engineering *any* voice. They can, in fact, reproduce the accent, intonation, and cadence of any given person with a modest recording of their speech (around 15 minutes or so). Early applications of this technology were demonstrated in 2017 on major politicians like Barack Obama, Hillary Clinton, and Donald Trump.

As this type of style transfer is adopted by near-human-level systems, numerous questions will begin to arise about the authenticity of audio recordings. This is a society-level discussion that we are—as a whole—ill-equipped to have today, and yet it will have massive repercussions.

Chapter 6

Use Cases for AI

Use cases sit at the top of the AI framework presented in this book. They rely on the applications and technologies that form the more technical AI models. Use cases are the most recognizable layer of the AI field to most people, as it's what they're exposed to in consumer-facing systems.

Just as with technologies and applications, the use cases presented in this book are not meant to compose an exhaustive list. Doing so would be impossible; new use cases are being invented on a daily basis. Rather, the intent here is to provide a bit of color on some of the more common and impactful use cases, as well as explore how technologies and applications can be packaged to effect real-world change.

The below use cases are (very) roughly organized from most immediately impactful to least, except where it makes sense to talk about related use cases together (e.g., gaming agents right after digital agents).

Autonomous vehicles

Very few AI use cases have captured the headlines like autonomous vehicles. And for good reason: their potential to disrupt the economy and society is massive. Whether for personal or commercial purposes, driving takes up a tremendous amount of time and energy; the potential to free up those resources at the scale of hundreds of millions of people is hard to fathom.

The technology driving autonomous vehicles has progressed substantially in the past decade. In 2007 at the DARPA Urban Challenge, competitors were given 6 hours to navigate a 60 mile course. Today, autonomous vehicles developed by a dozen different manufacturers are capable of navigating many city streets as fluently as any human driver.

The realistic possibilities of autonomous vehicles were perhaps best demonstrated with Google's driverless car program in the early 2010s. In more recent years, Tesla has released relatively basic autonomous technology that has by far the most adoption on the road today. Numerous auto manufacturers have targeted 2020 for the release of the first fully autonomous commercial vehicle, though there are still sub-problems that require refinement (like driving in poor visibility conditions or on bad roads).

The advancement of deep learning for computer vision has been critical to the optimism for autonomous vehicles over the past few years. However, most implementations still use a complex manually-defined expert system to connect various deep learning based applications operating at a lower level.

It is worth noting that while public conversation centers around wheeled vehicles, there is substantial work being done on aerial vehicles as well. Much of this was pioneered by the government for military drones, but more recently commercial drones have gained substantial traction. While regulations (and the technology) aren't quite there yet, many observers expect the first commercial autonomous drone deliveries within the next decade.

Robotics

Robotics is the general use case of software and hardware working in concert to navigate the physical world. Autonomous vehicles fall within this broader categorization. But there are a variety of specific use cases beyond autonomous vehicles where robotics have significant impact and potential.

To-date, the vast majority of real world impact from robotics has come in the industrial sector. Robotic manipulators and conveyors have seen significant traction in manufacturing settings, where in the U.S. there are currently around 15 robots for every 1,000 employees[8]. These robots have driven significant cost savings and improvement in quality and reliability. There has also been substantial adoption of robots in warehouse and distribution settings, as well-demonstrated by Amazon Robotics (formerly Kiva).

In industrial settings, robots are currently limited by their inability to manipulate arbitrary objects or navigate dynamic environments. Implementations must be very controlled and have little to no human presence. These requirements have led to substantial upfront cost of robotics implementations. Recent research, however, has focused on allowing robots to adapt to more natural environments. If this development sees substantial advancement, it could open up a much wider swath of the industry to disruption by robots.

Robotics has also begun to play a major role in surgeries in the healthcare industry. As a whole, robots have much more capability for reliable behavior and precision than human surgeons do. Today, implementations are still fairly limited and nearly always rely on a human operator. However, development efforts are focused on allowing robotic surgery devices to operate with more autonomy.

Consumer use cases for robotics have remained fairly niche. With the exception of Roomba-type vacuum cleaners, robots as a whole don't have the flexibility to operate in non-standardized environments. Again, current development focus is seeking to expand the environments where robots can practically be used. Likely short term uses include lawn mowing and rigid object manipulation (e.g., loading the dishwasher). Other objects, like clothes, are substantially harder for robots to work with; as such, it will likely still be some time before we see robotic clothes folders.

Digital agents

The software-only equivalent of robots are often referred to as digital agents. These agents are programmed to navigate relatively complex sets of tasks and often emulate the behavior of humans. They can operate in a number of different contexts and in some cases the dividing line between digital agents and other use cases of machine learning may not be completely clear.

Historically, the most common implementation of the digital agent was a chatbot. Some may remember experiments in this direction during the 1990s and 2000s (SmarterChild was one of the more popular ones). In many cases, these bots were little more than experiments in understanding natural language human-computer interfaces. Most provided little to no direct value for the users interacting with them.

Digital agents have seen a massive surge in development, interest, and value since the packaging of Siri as a standard iPhone feature in 2011. More recently, many other large tech companies (Google, Microsoft, Amazon) have introduced their own human-like digital assistant for basic consumer-oriented tasks. The tasks that these agents can perform are quite varied: book an Uber, answer basic knowledge questions, transcribe a text message from voice.

The currently dominant digital agents primarily rely on voice-to-text to convert their audio input and NLQ to understand what a user is asking (and then provide a response). Voice-to-text is fast becoming a solved problem, though there is still significant research on the application from each of the major tech companies. NLQ, on the other hand, is the primary bottleneck for faster agent development. Currently, each use case for the digital agents requires substantial manual programming, pattern recognition, and response templating. There is still next to no generalization within this domain.

There are a variety of other types of digital assistants beyond the type that have become integrated into smartphones and other types of computing devices. A large sub-category of these include chatbots that act as an interface between companies and their customers. These chatbots can sell products, answer questions, solve problems, and perform any one of many other actions that a customer might need. There was substantial optimism around the potential for chatbots to reshape customer service; almost none of that potential has been realized as of early 2018.

While thousands of companies have experimented with the chatbot medium, most implementations led to unacceptable levels of frustration for customers when they discovered how inflexible basic chatbot implementations were. While more dynamic agents are possible, they are generally still too expensive (requiring manual rule programming) to justify the investment for most companies.

Outside of chatbots, startups are experimenting with digital assistants to perform most types of digital actions. One of the more interesting uses is meeting scheduling. Simply copy the AI assistant as you would a human assistant, and it will take care of the back-and-forth communication to get a meeting on the calendar. Complex use cases like these are still far from being fully automated, but have the potential for significant economic disruption. They are also very valuable as an opportunity to implement so-called "human-in-the-loop" systems that depend on a combination of AI and humans to complete a task. In many cases, these hybrid systems can achieve economically advantageous results long before reaching true automation.

Gaming

A massive subset of digital agents encompasses programs written to play games. These include many of the most famous digital agents in AI's history: Deep Blue, AlphaGo, and Watson. Board games provided an attractive early goal for game-playing agent development. Board games are generally well-constrained, making them much easier for AI agents to play and eventually beat humans.

Basic games like tic-tac-toe and checkers are now "solved": they are so constrained that the perfect set of moves is known. More advanced games, like chess and go, still require problem solving and strategy. It is far more recent that computers have begun to dominate such games (the first software to defeat a professional go player was AlphaGo in 2015). Research in this domain is ongoing. The newer version of AlphaGo (AlphaZero) is now the top player in the world in both go and chess, and will almost certainly never be supplanted by a human.

Video games loom as the next major horizon for game-playing AI agents. Development in this field is decades-old:

simple rules-based systems have been prevalent since the very earliest games. Until recently, the rules-based approach has dominated in every single game type. DeepMind (the creators of AlphaGo) kicked off a new era of more advanced AI agents for games: their earliest creation was built to apply reinforcement learning to Atari games, achieving superhuman performance in many of them.

AI research is more interesting for some game types than others. The First Person Shooter (FPS) genre, for instance, already features AI programs that can defeat top humans in many games. That is because FPS games are highly reliant on precise aim and quick reaction speeds, both of which computers will always dominate. Games that are more rooted in strategy like the Real Time Strategy (RTS) and Multiplayer Online Battle Arena (MOBA) genres have historically been resistant to advanced AI programs. The number of viable options for gameplay is essentially intractable, limiting the effectiveness of decision- or policy-tree approaches that work well for games like chess and go.

In 2017 AI began to be competitive in certain subsets of these genres. OpenAI published the results of a program they had developed that could beat the world's top players at a very constrained version of the game Dota2, one of the most popular MOBA titles. While this constrained version was much easier than the general form of the game and doesn't fully represent how professionals play, it was the first sign that AI was on the verge of achieving human-level performance in even these more strategic game types. Then in early 2019, the OpenAI Five system defeated the world's top professional teams, moving Dota2 into the category of "solved" problem.

Search engines

While search engines don't typically stand out as a top use case of AI, the reality is that they have been making use of machine learning to improve their accuracy for years.

Google is notoriously tight-lipped about their page ranking algorithm, but some details have come to light over the years. One is that they take into account user behavior in identifying the most relevant results. For instance, if someone clicks into the 5th link for a given search and doesn't come back to the search page, Google might assume that their search was answered by that result. As a massive simplification, that result might bump up from 5th to 3rd the next time someone searches for the same query.

The reality of how Google (and other search engines) implement AI is far more complex. In recent years, they have begun to take more user-level context into account, factoring in your recent search queries and the general types of queries that you generally put in.

Search engines were one of the first major implementations of semantic processing within the application of NLP. The earliest search engines relied on what is known as "keyword search", just looking for the presence of the words you were searching for in the documents they were returning. These early efforts suffered from all of the challenges that the basic NLP applications mentioned in the Applications chapter see. To progress beyond that point, a decade or so ago Google pioneered an understanding of the interrelationships between the words in a search query to drive more accurate results.

Search engines provide an excellent case study for people first approaching the field of AI. First, it is a clear area where AI has been used for years without people realizing it. Even today, many people believe that AI has no real impact on their lives, while at the same time using Google on a near-hourly basis. Second, it is a good demonstration that the application of AI is sometimes completely non-transparent to the user. If Google hadn't opened up in bits and pieces about its methodology, you could still guess that they were relying on manual rules or some other form of algorithm that couldn't be considered AI at all. This is a useful lesson for the field of AI overall: in many cases, the outcome of the algorithm is what matters, not which specific model is used to accomplish it.

Investing

While not visible to most people, the world of investing actually drove much of the early economic impact of AI. In equities investing, the application of AI essentially began when NASDAQ introduced digital trading in the early 1980s.

While there is no good categorization in the equities investment industry for the application of AI, much of the technology behind "high-frequency trading" (HFT) could be considered AI of some sort. HFT relies on high-speed digital communications to make trades faster than a human could process the same information. At its most basic, HFT is about avoiding some of the costs that come with slow trade processing times. However, more advanced funds utilizing HFT have sophisticated algorithms for parsing data and making independent trade decisions using logic similar to what a human would do if they had the time.

Broadly, HFT belongs to a broader category of "algorithmic trading". Algorithmic trading began as the digitization of a human process: conducting trades in pieces according to basic rules around timing, volume, and pricing. Algorithmic trading was originally developed as a way to minimize cost and risk. However, the applications of AI for independent decision making around investments end up looking very similar to this technology in many cases.

The world of investing provides an interesting lens into the adoption patterns for advanced technologies like AI. Equities trading is a cut-throat industry where razor-thin advantages can make all the difference. Early applications of AI provided exactly these types of advantages: perhaps not massively better or more automated than human analysis, but enough so to justify the investment. It is possible that other industries would benefit from a similarly quick feedback loop and visibility into the benefits of minor improvements.

Medical diagnosis

The healthcare industry is a particularly difficult space for AI to grab a foot hold: most new technologies must undergo very thorough scrutiny before being accepted for commercial use. For technology like AI, where substantial innovation is happening on a near-daily basis, the implementations in healthcare must necessarily lag other industries by at least a year or two.

That being said, there has been significant interest in applying AI technologies in medical diagnosis. While still somewhat limited in an every-day hospital setting, these implementations have seen some promising early results.

The most common use for AI in diagnosis is for medical imaging. Imaging includes x-rays, CT scans, MRIs, and ultrasounds. Historically, doctors examine these images manually and attempt to diagnose potential issues. These manual evaluations have substantial variation from doctor to doctor, leading to inconsistency in diagnosis. Early applications of computer vision to these images show significant potential for standardizing analysis and improving accuracy over time.

Although not as developed as medical imaging, there is another use of AI for diagnosis based on text data. Over the past decade or so, health systems have begun to standardize their digital health record keeping. This information is a rich set of data for machine learning algorithms that can process doctors' notes and tie them to the ultimate diagnosis and outcome. The possibilities are fascinating: an objective approach that is not subject to the biases of individual doctors, more accurate and early diagnosis, and treatment plans that many result in better outcomes.

Education

The education field has been experimenting with basic uses of AI for decades. Much of this effort has focused on adaptive testing: adjusting the difficulty of questions as a student proceeds through an evaluation based on how they are doing. This form of dynamic questioning and scoring is now the norm for many standardized tests in the United States.

At its most basic, adaptive testing only barely qualifies as AI. The idea is simple: assign each question a difficulty score and serve up harder questions if the student is doing well. There is some interesting work around how "doing well" is defined, but the basic version of the problem is fairly simple.

There are, however, more advanced forms of adaptive testing that are more impressive from a technical perspective. Rather than a question having a simple difficulty score, the question can exist more as a vector of difficulties, with each dimension of the vector representing some specific type of knowledge or skill. The adaptive test can then guide a student toward the area within a complex domain where they may need more attention.

Although it has received the most attention to-date, adaptive testing is just a part of a larger paradigm of adaptive education. AI can be incredibly useful in the *delivery* of learning material, not just the evaluation of knowledge. Broadly, these solutions are known as "Intelligent Tutoring Systems" (ITS).

Similar to adaptive testing, the ITS approach tailors delivery and the content itself according to the student's needs. In doing so it is mimicking the behavior of a human tutor: providing a customized learning path that is optimized for the individual student. This approach is far more effective than the general mass pedagogical model used in most classrooms, which typically has to accommodate the lowest common denominator. In limited testing, ITSs have shown substantial improvement in education outcomes over more traditional education models.

The main constraining factor on adaptive testing and adaptive education overall is the human labor that goes into creating the systems. For an ITS, the rule of thumb is that each hour of educational content requires about 100 hours of labor to prepare because there are so many possible paths that the student can take. While this equation can be economical when applied at scale, most efforts so far have been stymied by the high upfront costs. Using AI to automate the content creation step of system development is an active area of research and is likely the key to widespread adoption of the adaptive education paradigm.

Tailored advertising

Similar to investment use cases, advertising drove a substantial amount of early commercial AI use outside of the general perception of consumers. Google is responsible for a great deal of the advancement in advertising technologies, though its sophistication is now matched (and in some ways surpassed) by Facebook.

The role of AI in digital advertising is to serve up ads that are more relevant to a given user. When done right, this should result in a higher likelihood for the user to act on the ad—and drive a desirable outcome for the creator of the ad.

This user-level customization typically takes in attributes of the user such as their demographics (age, gender, location, etc.) and internet usage behavior. Logically, this information can be used in a similar way to recommendation engines (in some ways, an advertisement is a sponsored recommendation) to maximize the likelihood of the user finding the ad relevant.

Along with pushing the technology, early advertising uses also gave rise to questions around data privacy. There was a famous case of a father finding out his daughter was pregnant when Target sent her targeted advertisement for new baby products based on her behavior. These types of intelligent advertising are now ubiquitous: essentially all internet users come across ads for flights they were looking at, shoes they thought about buying, or from websites they visited once. While targeting is innocuous in most cases, there are serious risks of overstepping the boundaries of reasonable privacy, resulting in serious negative outcomes for consumers.

Media recommendation

Of all of the uses of AI, recommendation systems for media consumption may have the most impact on the general population. Netflix pioneered the field in the late 2000s, even going so far as to host a public multi-year competition to improve their algorithms.

Today, AI is used for recommendations on all types of media: articles, books, songs, TV, and movies. Netflix has one of the top implementations, but similar systems have been built by hundreds of providers (Amazon, YouTube, Spotify, Hulu, Medium, Twitter, etc.).

In just the past decade or so, media consumption has shifted from self-selection and human curation to being largely driven by AI recommendations. This phenomenon has led to concerns that society is dividing itself into bubbles of influence based on people's current preferences. If AI is only serving up content that you're familiar with and know you want to consume, then by definition your exposure to new ideas and perspectives decreases.

Product recommendation

Recommendation systems for products work very similar to systems for media: the system takes in information about a user's preferences and habits then spits out a list of products that it believes the user is most likely to be interested in purchasing.

In some ways product recommendation is a much more challenging problem than media recommendation; the world of possible products that someone might be interested in purchasing is much wider than the media they might want to consume (in fact, the product set probably includes much of the media set). However, the payoff for getting the recommendation right is that much more valuable—accurate product recommendations can drive substantial increases in revenue and profitability for retailers. This is essentially the gold at the end of the rainbow for all sales and marketing efforts. If you can convince a customer to give you money for something they otherwise wouldn't, then you can justify substantial expense in the process. Of course, there is an obvious argument to be made that the consumer benefits as well, discovering a product that will make their life better.

No company has invested more heavily in building advanced product recommendation algorithms than Amazon. And that makes sense: they have the lion's share of the online retail market and therefore an unparalleled opportunity to profit from product recommendations (although product recommendation is possible in non-digital environments, it is not nearly as natural there). Amazon stumbled on the power of AI fairly early in its company history, discovering in its first few years that the scales it operated at didn't lend themselves to hand-curated recommendations made by humans.

Product recommendation systems share much in common with tailored advertising algorithms. In each case, the software takes in data about a consumer and tries to get them to spend time or money where they otherwise wouldn't. Accordingly, those who stand to benefit from greater product recommendation accuracy—like Amazon—invest heavily in getting as much data about their customers as they reasonably can. Amazon's proprietary data (your purchase history) provides a strong signal, but they can make ever-more-accurate recommendations as they learn about their customers' age, geography, ethnicity, and a host of other personal information.

Cybersecurity

AI plays a large—and growing—role in cybersecurity. As digital systems grow in complexity, their vulnerabilities tend to expand in lock-step. Systems today are a couple of orders of magnitude more complex than earlier networked systems from just a decade or two ago. They have long-since become too complex for any single human to understand all of the details of even a medium-sized network. And due to the interdependencies of the various technologies in the network, there are often gaps in the ability for even a team of people to fully comprehend all of the ways that their network might be compromised.

The primary role of AI in cybersecurity is processing sets of data too large for humans to comprehend. While AI still doesn't have the type of intuition or problem solving needed to generate a holistic defense for an IT system, it can be invaluable as a layer of security or a tool to accomplish a specific task.

One of the most common applications of AI in cybersecurity is anomaly detection: establishing a baseline pattern of behavior for a system and then flagging to a human reviewer when behavior deviates from that standard. Many types of system infiltration generate signatures that would not show up in normal usage of the system: a million login attempts in the span of a minute or a user accessing a set of information they have no reason to need.

AI can also be used to automate time-intensive manual processes, like penetration testing. Algorithms have been used for this work (i.e., scanning every port to see which ones will accept traffic) for years, but more recently additional intelligence has been layered on to identify ever-more-sophisticated vulnerabilities. This type of automated approach scales almost infinitely. As such, it is often used for non-targeted attacks: scanning a large chunk of the internet for vulnerabilities without having any one target in mind. Although less direct than target attacks, this approach can still have massive consequences. There was an infamous incident in 2017 where hundreds of millions of records on American voters were compromised by this sort of approach.

It is worth mentioning that AI is playing a leading role in the development of more advanced "black-hat" hacking approaches as well. This hacking is the flip side of cybersecurity: the bad actors attempt to penetrate technology systems for their own gain. While there is a clear moral divide between the "white-hat" methodologies used to secure systems and black-hat hacking, the technology itself tends to look very similar.

In 2016, the DARPA Cyber Grand Challenge featured the first all-AI hacking competition. Each competing team was an entirely autonomous piece of software that received no human input once the competition began: developing attacks and defenses on their own. While technologies like this are still not commonplace, the competition serves as a harbinger for where the industry is headed. As a reminder, it will be less than 15 years after the DARPA Urban Grand Challenge when the first fully autonomous commercial car is released.

Document review (legal)

The magnitude of potential impact for AI on the legal industry is hard to overestimate. In fact, the impact is already being felt: the application of "predictive coding" is quickly becoming widespread. Predictive coding automates document classification during the discovery phase of the litigation process. Where attorneys would previously have been required to manually review each document, now computer programs can quickly categorize thousands in seconds.

Although predictive coding is the first major adoption of AI for automation in the legal industry, it's just the tip of the iceberg. Several startups are developing technology to automate more general legal document review. These systems can flag unusual contract terms, identify contradictory or non-compliant passages, or do any of the other myriad basic tasks that previously required manual review by an attorney at $400 per hour.

A couple of startups have also experimented with automating legal paperwork filing. One notable system in London reversed thousands of parking tickets that didn't meet the proper citation requirements. Similarly, AI can help automate small business regulatory filings, community-led political petitions, and any number of other complicated processes that were previously toll-gated behind a need for niche expertise and knowledge.

Smart image analytics/search

One of the watershed moments of this current AI revolution was in 2015 when AI first achieved human-level performance at identifying objects in images as part of the ImageNet competition. This period heralded unparalleled interest and research into the use of deep neural networks for image processing, a technology that had previously seen limited success in OCR and autonomous robotics technologies.

In just the few years since the ImageNet success, the amount of technology applied to image processing has exploded. Every major cloud provider now has a commercial service for labeling images that performs at a reasonable level of accuracy (though the systems are still far from perfect and their errors are often inhumanly humorous). Google and Facebook now have massive, accurate databases of people's faces. Computer vision based systems are now the dominant solution for loss prevention for retailers: automatic flagging of "suspicious" behavior from store cameras replacing historical investment in secret shoppers patrolling the store by foot.

Over the past couple of years, intelligent image analysis has become more and more prevalent in consumer use cases. Most people have now had the moment of astonishment when their Google Photos or Apple Photos are sorted in some kind of intuitive fashion that they did not establish themselves ("pictures at the beach", "pictures of your dog"). This can be quickly explored through Google's Image Search by searching for something remarkably specific, like "pink flower with 8 petals". Google's results are astonishingly accurate, particularly when you realize there's no way humans have labeled billions of photos with this type of information.

The broader commercial application for smart image analytics is still very much in the exploration phase. Some early use cases have been found for satellite imagery. The insurance industry uses this information to assess broad geographic risk and to verify individual-level information (like whether or not a given customer has a pool in their backyard). The finance industry has also explored the opportunity in depth: using imagery to automatically assess levels of oil reserves or projected yield of crops.

The possibilities for intelligent image analysis are only just beginning to be explored in a wide range of other fields. One idea is to use it for automated visual testing of web application development. Another is to generate a type of narration for movies that can explain a scene to someone who is blind. Yet another is to monitor patients or study participants in a healthcare environment for compliance on a physical therapy or medicine regimen.

While for many corporations their text-based documents are likely the richest source of value for AI-driven unstructured data processing, image analysis is probably the second most valuable, with much of the potential still unexplored.

Professional development

The application of AI to professional development has emerged as a top use case over the past two years or so. This evolved out of early analytics-based approaches to roles that lended themselves to quantification: sales, certain types of marketing, low-cost software development. These functions pushed the boundaries of how much human managerial oversight was needed to optimize the performance of large teams.

Before diving into how AI is being applied in a more general way today, it is worth acknowledging that there have been many missteps and unnecessary pain as a result of the push to automate professional development in these early groups. Removing human judgment and holding employees accountable to a simple set of numbers introduces all kinds of perverse incentives that can hurt company performance. These missteps have led to a great deal of advancement in how companies approach this type of professional development, and it is important that these lessons carry over to more advanced automated professional development driven by AI.

Much of the information economy has resisted automation of management and professional development because the underlying data was unstructured: most of a knowledge worker's work product shows up in written or spoken words. The rise of AI for processing unstructured data has introduced the possibility of automation where it didn't previously exist.

Applications in this realm start at the very basic: analyzing the professionalism of emails, for instance. An automated system can flag to an employee when their email could use some polishing up (maybe just a single exclamation point instead of five). For workers whose jobs center on this type of communication, there is the possibility of basing more longitudinal feedback and review on this metric. An email-based customer service representative, for instance, might—in-part— be rated on the average level of courtesy in their emails to customers.

More advanced AI-driven professional development can be used as a tool for root-cause analysis of performance anomalies. While often not enough to indicate good or poor performance on its own, this anomaly detection might be able to diagnose bad performance as a product of a worker spending too much time doing Google searches or writing emails too slowly relative to their peers.

There are very few viable uses of AI today for direct evaluation or prescription of improvement for knowledge workers. Be wary of solutions that promise this kind of automation. For now, AI should still be considered one tool in providing high quality professional development and managerial review.

Predictive maintenance

Although constrained to the industrial sector, few use cases of AI have seen earlier or more economically impactful implementations than predictive maintenance. Predictive maintenance involves pattern recognition and anomaly detection to drive just-in-time maintenance for machines (like a CNC mill or a locomotive). Given enough data, such a system can distinguish between vibration that's within acceptable range and the type of shaking in one subsystem that means the entire machine will soon have a catastrophic failure.

Predictive maintenance is an evolution from the classic maintenance paradigms of reactive (fix it when it breaks) and preventative (fix things on a schedule so they never break). It balances the efficiency of reactive (don't fix things too soon) with the uptime of preventative (don't fix things too late). It has been applied over the past decade in essentially every corner of the industrial economy: manufacturing, power generation, transportation, etc.

The impact of a successful predictive maintenance can be massive. A 747 that is grounded for unexpected maintenance can cost an airline millions of dollars and disrupt an entire region's operations. Reducing the rate of such incidents even marginally can drive enormous savings. This is just as true for any high value asset, like a gas turbine or a key piece of machinery in an automotive plant.

Voice-of-the-customer analytics

An early use case for unstructured data processing was in assessing the opinions of customers en masse through analysis of their communications with the company. This use case ("voice-of-the-customer analytics" or "text analytics") sought to generate insights at a scale that couldn't be achieved through human review: it is difficult for any person to pull out a consistent thread across a million chat logs without several layers of abstraction.

These early uses revolved around two NLP applications: sentiment analysis and topic identification. The idea was that the system would automatically break transcripts into a set of the most common topics, then assess whether the customer generally felt positively or negatively about those topics. This technology could be used by a consumer bank—for instance—to understand that customers loved their free checking but thought their interest rates on savings accounts were too low.

The commercial application of these technologies was limited by bad AI transcription for phone call logs and basic NLP that didn't leverage semantic analysis. Although the insights weren't typically wrong, they lacked the specificity and nuance necessary to be immediately actionable.

In recent years, the potential for these systems has massively increased along with the ability for AI to process unstructured information. Voice-to-text is now largely accurate and semantic-based NLP has become far more accessible. In addition, the amount of information to process the voice of the customer has exploded with sites like Yelp, TripAdvisor, and Twitter.

The main challenge for business professionals looking to implement advanced voice-of-the-customer analytics is distinguishing between the basic legacy systems and their more recent advanced successors. Most of the difference advertised by providers is just marketing; truly understanding the differences requires an in-depth review of each technology on real data to see how it performs.

Article writing

Article writing is one of the few use cases of nascent NLG AI applications. Specifically, AI is now in limited use for writing news articles and digests of corporate financial reports. While writing overall is an AI-hard problem that will not be solved in the near future, AI can perform reasonably well in highly constrained circumstances.

One of these circumstances is for sports reporting. In many cases, these types of articles follow a fairly standard template: who won a game, what the scores were, breakdowns by period, breakdowns by individual athlete. Given the templatized nature, AI can translate a stat sheet into natural language that is easier to digest for a broad audience. This type of automated sports journalism has already been used for some high-volume, high-profile events (like the Olympics or the World Cup).

Automated article writing is also being used for synthesizing corporate financial reports. The periodic reports generated by companies often follow a standard template, lending themselves to automated processing. Once the information is structured, it can then be repackaged into natural language for broad consumption. Such an article could report on the basics: Apple's quarterly revenue and profit, broken down by geography or product line. The articles might also do some basic explanation: highlighting that unexpectedly low revenue was driven by overly-optimistic projections for sales of the most recent iPhone.

While there are claims that AI is writing more complicated or creative works, those claims must generally be taken with a grain of salt. Although it is true that there are AI-written novels, poems, and screenplays, they are not quite the same as the fully automated articles based on standard templates. Generally they require some level of human input in the creation process and a large amount of curation on the tail-end (a poem might be the best of a hundred written by the same program).

AI will typically not be a helpful technology in writing for most corporations. There are, however, some uses where AI can provide substantial cost savings. If—for some reason—a company requires a large number of reports to be documented in natural language (a construction company's daily site reports, for instance), AI can potentially be used to translate form-based notes into long-form. Unfortunately, such efforts are often impractical. The expertise to develop such a system isn't nearly as prevalent as it is for other common commercial uses of AI technology (like more general NLP).

Audio transcription

As mentioned elsewhere in this book, the capabilities of AI voice-to-text applications have improved substantially over the past few years. There are numerous claims of human-level accuracy by the major technology players. This advancement has opened up substantial opportunity in the field of audio transcription.

Accurate voice-to-text is key to voice-of-the-customer analytics applied to call centers (as the phone calls must be converted to text transcripts). Transcription might also be used for automatically documenting meetings and conference calls, though that use case has not been thoroughly explored in the real world due to the historical inaccuracy of previous systems. The potential for these use cases is still not fully explored.

More advanced technology is now being used for companies who make transcription their product, like Rev. These companies have provided ad-hoc transcription services for the professional and academic worlds, where each transcript is generated manually by humans earning an hourly wage. These companies are now experimenting with automating the process, though the technology has not quite reached human levels of accuracy. As such, the current evolving paradigm involves a hybrid approach of an initially-generated AI transcript followed by human review.

As the technology advances, the companies will likely be forced to make semi-professional transcription services available on more of an on-demand consumer model. Perhaps the transcripts won't come with a professional level of polish, but will be available virtually instantly at a tenth of the cost.

Chapter 7

When and How to Use AI

Now that you have an introduction to what artificial intelligence actually *means* and the various technologies that compose it, you can begin thinking about how to apply AI in *your* world.

A note if you have skipped straight to this chapter, passing over the previous four: this chapter on its own probably won't do you much good. That's because trying to implement an AI solution without understanding it doesn't make much sense. While a non-technical manager can safely defer to their technical comrades on questions like "Python or Node.js" (actually, for AI it should probably be Python), the business outcomes of a given application of AI are too closely tied to the technologies used; all stakeholders must thoroughly understand the full context.

Know what you're talking about

So let's call that lesson number one of using AI: know what you're talking about. Don't be the manager that nods along vacantly when the software contractor says they'll be using a ConvNet for their unsupervised clustering model. The field is too new and the industry as a whole too uninformed: not doing your research before undertaking an AI project is the first step toward failure.

The good news is that this book is a terrific starting resource. A base level of familiarity with the content of this book will immediately put you above at least 90% of your non-technical colleagues. This book is also meant to be a helpful reference resource: when you come across a term covered in the book that you've since forgotten, simply come back and get reacquainted. Most of the similar resources you will find online were built for technical people; they mostly won't explain concepts and terms with the same kind of context you'll find here.

That is, however, your next stop. If you can't remember the difference between a ConvNet and an RNN or want to know why you would use LSTM over a more conventional RNN (which doesn't get much attention in this book), the internet is often going to be your best resource. I would even recommend this kind of self-study over consulting a technical colleague; again, there is just so much misinformation floating around that you should be careful in who you decide to trust for expertise.

When searching the internet for your AI-related questions, source matters a lot. While Wikipedia will typically be one of the top results, it's probably not where you want to start. The AI content on Wikipedia is often too technical and too detailed for the purposes of a non-technical professional looking for an introduction to a topic. Instead, try searching for things like "an introduction to deep learning" or "what problems is random forest good for".

As you undertake problems in the AI world, you will probably find yourself lost a lot. It's a big and complicated field. Much of the terminology hasn't even standardized yet. Don't let that frustrate you; much of the source of that frustration is the price we pay for the rapid advancement we're seeing today. The reward for gaining that knowledge is the ability to solve problems that we couldn't even think of addressing with software a decade or two ago.

Choose the right difficulty level

In video games, you may be asked what difficulty level you would like to play at. "Easy" is for someone just looking to kill some time and have a pleasurable experience. "Insane" is for skilled and experienced gamers who get excited by the challenge of the game (instead of the graphics, plot, or other more casual elements). Top difficulty levels are often for gamers who have played the game once on a lower level and are looking to get even more entertainment value from a second play-through.

Keep these difficulty levels in mind as you think about where and how you would like to apply AI in your business. If you're just beginning to explore what AI has to offer and don't have much of an appetite for risk, you may want to start on "easy" mode: out-of-the-box applications of pre-built AI tools deployed on well-studied use cases. That might look like sentiment analysis on customer reviews or automatic language translation for a specific business tool. The cloud-based AI services offered by Google, Microsoft, and others are perfect for these basic use cases.

Unsurprisingly, there is tremendous potential value locked away in the more difficult levels of AI. Object detection and intelligent search of images often lives in what might be called the "Medium" difficulty level. "Hard" might be a use case like a free-form chatbot or an autonomous agent that attempts to optimize your business processes without much direction. Medium and hard use cases will typically require significant in-house expertise and custom development work. In many cases, you may be exploring the cutting-edge of the technology in places where a viable solution may not even exist.

It is important to be honest with yourself about what difficulty level you're prepared to be "playing" at. If your mandate is to innovate and explore new technology, you may have the risk tolerance to jump into the deep end with use cases that may prove intractable in the short term. If you're attempting to push technology in a more traditional corporation, you may want to prove out small wins with easy use cases before attempting to make the business case for riskier solutions with higher potential upsides.

Find the right problems

For most software projects, thoroughly understanding the problem is often more important than a well-planned-out solution. That principle is doubly true for problems where you aspire to apply AI. As new AI technologies get invented on a monthly basis, much of the commercial potential for AI isn't fully understood.

Businesses across industries all over the world are experimenting with the application of AI technologies to new use cases; some will work fantastically, others will fail miserably. Much of the key to setting yourself up for success lies in knowing which problems may lend themselves to an AI solution.

Automation

If you believe that AI is the use of software to mimic human capabilities, then it stands to reason that one of the main business purposes of AI solutions would be to automate the existing behavior of human workers. And indeed, there are many cases where automating manual work is the perfect use of AI.

Of course, not just any work can be automated away by software today. For better or worse, AI still can't replicate the complexity of human problem solving and intelligence in the general sense.

I've heard the potential for AI in automation described as a bit of a thought exercise: "If you had 10,000 interns, what would you do with them?". I don't love the line of thinking that you can have interns do any drudge work you want, but the underlying premise is still sound: AI is generally quite good at doing massive amounts of very low-skill and repetitive work. These types of work include digitizing large numbers of physical documents, reading thousands of customer reviews and interviews to pull out primary topics, and executing financial transactions based on relatively well-defined rules.

Just as with interns, you shouldn't expect your AI algorithms to execute complex tasks requiring advanced judgment and significant business context. AI just isn't that smart yet.

Monitoring/Search

As many managers have learned the hard way, just because a task doesn't require much cognition doesn't mean that it can be solved by large amounts of unskilled labor. Pattern recognition or anomaly detection on large datasets is a surprisingly tricky problem for humans to address. Imagine staring at a list of numbers scrolling by hour after hour, every day for weeks. The specific number you're looking for may only show up once a year. It's hard to fault the poor soul tasked with staring at the screen if they miss the number after hours of noise.

Machines, on the other hand, are perfectly suited to this task. They don't get tired, they don't get distracted. Their eyesight doesn't get blurry after looking at a stream of numbers for 10 hours straight. That's why software is much better than humans at continuous monitoring or mass-search activities.

Still, even the most advanced AI methods are fairly limited in their ability to identify complex patterns without direction, particularly when those patterns rely on outside context. As with automation, keep your expectations for the "intelligence" of the AI solution fairly low.

Superhuman

Many might consider the two previous types of problem to be suitable for "dumb" AI: relatively simple rule sets applied at scale (that can admittedly have significant business impact). More and more, problems are being identified that can be tackled by new types of more intelligent AI: algorithms that can achieve greater-than-human performance on specific tasks.

For a full listing of these specific problems, check the **"Conquered" AI Problems** section at the end of this book. They include tasks like facial recognition, object recognition in images, and now (or soon) voice-to-text transcription. These are tasks that were best categorized as "automation" even a few years ago, with the caveat that you were losing accuracy by allowing software to tackle the problem instead of humans. With recent advancements, however, software can now achieve better results than low-skill workforces.

These types of problems require the most consideration before attempting a solution. For instance, while voice-to-text algorithms may now (or soon) be able to achieve superhuman performance, that may come with the caveat that the voice you're transcribing must have an American-neutral accent. If the speaker has a thick Eastern European accent, the performance of the software may drop to well below human level.

When attempting superhuman application of AI, it is often a good idea to under-promise on the outcomes of the project. There is simply too much risk in promising theoretical superhuman outcomes based on limited applications; the technologies are often too new to understand the full scope of when those results may be possible.

Find the right solution

Once you have a problem that you understand well and that you really believe is well-suited to an AI-oriented solution, it's time to start thinking about how you're going to solve it.

The first thing to keep in mind is that AI is rarely a solution *on its own*. Rather, an AI model will most often be the focal point for a much larger software solution. My own software company provides a perfect example: one of our core AI models helps our users prioritize how often they should be following up with their contacts. This is however, just a small piece of a much broader onboarding experience, most of which doesn't rely on AI in the slightest. In fact, of the few thousand lines of code dedicated to the 4Degrees onboarding, only around a hundred or so could be considered real AI.

With that in mind, the details of the AI itself are critically important to the success of the overall solution. For the prioritization model I mentioned above, we knew from the beginning that we wouldn't be using deep learning; the scale of the training data required was simply impractical for an early stage startup. We had competing hypotheses on the efficacy of a regression- or classification-based approach, so tested them both. Among classifiers, we knew that logistic regression, a support vector machine, or a random forest were likely our best bet based on the type of data and predictions we were looking to make, so we didn't waste any time trying to shape a naive Bayes model to what we were trying to do.

The type of solution you're looking for will depend a lot on the specific problem and on the difficulty level that you've selected. If you're playing on Easy, then most of the technical details mentioned in the previous paragraph won't matter to you; they'll be abstracted away by the use of a cloud AI platform. It's important to have expertise on the project that is directly related to the type of solution that you're building.

Building the right team

Depending on the type of AI solution that you're building, the types of professionals that you'll want on your team may vary widely. Many consulting firms are beginning to learn how they can apply the out-of-the-box offerings of cloud solutions commercially. If you have a problem that is well-suited to a pre-built solution, then these consulting firms may be the perfect partner in helping make sure your project is a success. If, however, you are building something that requires a more bespoke solution, then you'll need to find practitioners with much deeper technical expertise (a much rarer skill set with a higher price tag).

It is worth bearing in mind that you may need to make some upfront investment in expertise to even *figure out* what type of team you will need. My advice would be to over-invest at this stage: a true expert in the field will be able to identify the right approach based on your organization's sophistication and the shape of the problem. Remember: to a hammer, everything looks like a nail. If you bring in one of the consulting firms that specializes in implementing solutions from a cloud service, then they will almost certainly find a way that your problem can be "perfectly" solved by that cloud service.

The next chapter focuses on the various types of professionals that may be helpful in attempting an AI solution. While your natural inclination may be to bring in AI technical experts and generalists for the other roles on the team, keep in mind that managing an AI project and designing an AI solution are just as specialized as writing the actual code.

The importance of data

Given that much of the power in AI technologies available today comes from machine learning, it is worth paying special attention to the data aspects of the project you're undertaking. The availability of existing datasets and the cost of generating your own will likely be major factors in the approach that you ultimately decide to take.

One of the reasons that companies like Google and Facebook have emerged at the forefront of deep learning development is because they have the massive amounts of data necessary for deep neural network training. If your organization or group isn't blessed with a significant portion of the data that exists on the internet, you may need to be a bit more realistic in your expectations for applying (or developing) cutting edge models.

If you have the time for it, one of the best approaches in AI development is often to start with the least data intense models and then evolve according to the problems you're running into. This first step may be a mini expert system: a small set of manually-defined rules that will begin to give you results. You may then layer on a basic classifier, which may work with as few as 100 data points. Just because some of the tech elite believe only deep learning is "real AI" doesn't mean that you need to scrap a project because you don't have 1,000,000 data points.

In some cases, however, the "start small and iterate" approach may not be viable. That approach may work with structured data or text but be completely untenable for rich media like photos or video. If you're working with this type of data, it may just be a reality that you need 10,000+ well-tagged data points before beginning to develop your model.

Timeline

One of the most important aspects of implementing AI solutions to many project managers is what impact the advanced technology might have on their project timelines. This is a very valid concern: all but the most basic AI implementations will require a different approach to timeline planning than standard software projects.

Like all applications of data science, developing AI can be frustrating to those who are accustomed to implementing more straightforward types of software. This is because effort spent against building AI may not always result in a product: instead, AI development can be thought of as a series of experiments. You form hypotheses about what approaches to the problem will work, collect data, implement a potential solution, and then measure your results. A natural part of this approach is that some of your experiments won't work out.

The implication for the manager's timeline is that it may make sense to bake in some buffer time for failed experiments. Assuming your first attempt will be successful is a recipe for missed deadlines. Additionally, when forming the project plan it may make sense to front-load as much of the experimentation as possible. After all, it's always possible that your experiments are all unsuccessful and the project is just not feasible; the fewer resources you can expend in that discovery the better.

Chapter 8

Types of AI Professionals

The surge in interest in artificial intelligence over the past few years has led to the emergence of new categories of AI professionals: people whose job it is to make the promise of AI a reality in the world. These tend to look like existing roles, simply adapted to the needs of implementing a specific type of advanced technology. Because the potential value of AI solutions is so high and the requisite expertise is so rare, these roles tend to command a premium in compensation.

Technical

As with the application of AI in the professional world as a whole, there is little standardization in terminology among AI roles. A data scientist at one company may be filling the exact same role as a machine learning engineer at another. Just as everyone has a different definition of AI, people tend to think about the connotations of a given AI title a bit differently and structure their organization accordingly.

The definitions presented here are only one perspective, though I believe that they reflect one of the more common approaches to defining the roles. If the specific meaning of these roles is important in the context of your professional work, you should make sure to spend time up front aligning all stakeholders on the specific meanings of the terms you are using.

Data Scientist

Data Scientist is one of the most common titles for people associated with the technical implementation of artificial intelligence. The downside of this prevalence is that it's also the least well-defined. Data Scientist has been used since well before machine learning was prevalent in the professional world and doesn't necessarily imply any kind of advanced AI work.

At its core the Data Scientist role is concerned with exactly what it sounds like: an advanced and rigorous approach to the use of data in the enterprise. This often just means statistical analysis, which mostly falls outside the realm of AI. To complicate matters further, plenty of organizations use the Data Scientist title for a role that would be better classified as "Analytics" in most settings: relatively basic data processing far more concerned with generating business insight than with parsing data in any kind of rigorous fashion.

With the rise of AI's popularity, it is becoming more common to use Data Scientist as the title for a role primarily concerned with implementing AI solutions. In that context, the Data Scientist role primarily connotes two things: 1) relatively ad hoc processing of data and 2) a more academic approach to data. Companies like Uptake thrive on the use of Data Scientists to generate one-off insights for their clients, similar to a consulting model.

Machine Learning Engineer

As both a title and a role, Machine Learning Engineer is newer than Data Scientist. As the name implies, ML Engineers apply machine learning technologies to develop AI systems. In comparison with Data Scientists, ML Engineers are often expected to be working more directly with software product and thinking about integrating machine learning into a continuously-operating system (not ad hoc).

Today, there are still many more general Software Engineers making extensive use of machine learning and other types of AI than there are specific Machine Learning Engineers. The divide between the two is far from clear: there are plenty of Software Engineers who are more adept at developing AI than junior ML Engineers. However, it is likely that the ML Engineer title becomes more prominent as it becomes more necessary for companies to distinguish the skill set (and the resulting increase in compensation).

As you consider AI engineers and their roles, it is worth remembering that machine learning is just a set of tools to achieve a given outcome. In many cases, more conventional AI may provide a better (or acceptable) outcome with a much simpler solution. Use of the Machine Learning Engineer title runs the risk of pigeon-holing your technical employees into a given approach, when it may not be the optimal one. This is often best addressed informally: making it clear that the outcome is what matters, not the technical details of the solution.

Researcher

The AI Researcher role is far less common than Data Scientists or Machine Learning Engineers, but is critical in organizations that are seeking to develop novel forms of AI. Google, Facebook, Microsoft, and nearly all of the autonomous vehicle companies hire large numbers of these types of researchers. In most cases, they are pulled from the academic community with the promise of substantially higher salaries (seven figures, in some cases) and the opportunity for real-world impact.

When you hear about the scarcity of AI talent in the world, it is true nowhere more than with researchers. While there are now thousands of engineers who can successfully apply deep neural networks, there are only a couple of hundred with the capability to develop truly novel models to solve new kinds of problems. The most prominent of these researchers have achieved celebrity-like status in the AI community (Yann LeCun, Andrew Ng, Yoshua Bengio), can command astronomical salaries, and are given large teams to work with by the tech giants.

In evaluating the skill needs of your organization, it is important to be thoughtful about how novel you really want to be in your approach. While you cannot build the types of advanced AI required to solve completely new problems (like driving a car through a city), the vast majority of corporations don't need anywhere near that advanced a skillset to successfully apply AI to their business.

It is also worth noting that AI Researchers cannot be expected to operate in isolation. Despite their high compensation, they will need a team of engineers to put their experiments into practice and ultimately convert their research into products.

Non-technical

To-date, most of the focus on new types of roles within the AI ecosystem have been on the technical side of the equation. More time has been spent thinking about the difference between a Data Scientist and a Machine Learning Engineer than about all of the details of non-technical roles combined. As such—in my opinion—more opportunity has been lost in cultivating good talent in the non-technical aspects of AI projects.

Because people tend to focus on the advanced technical requirements of AI projects, they tend to settle for non-technical team members with little to no AI experience. This leads to greater cost and lower likelihood of success because AI projects present a unique set of challenges that general professionals would not have experienced before. To implement AI in your organization successfully, it is important to consider the AI-specific experience of *all* of the members of the team, not just the technical team members.

Consultant

The most common non-technical AI role today is in the consulting world. Specialty firms like Element AI have arisen to provide exactly this kind of expertise. Nearly every global consulting firm has created an AI practice within the past few years with a similar (though less advanced) offering.

AI consultants provide critical value for corporations. This book was written because the in-depth knowledge required for the successful implementation of AI solutions is still incredibly rare throughout the professional world. While ideally companies will cultivate this kind of expertise internally, there is a lot to be said for the value of bringing in outside experts, particularly as an interim solution until the internal capabilities can be built.

As with all types of consulting, AI consultants bring in knowledge that a company doesn't have internally. This can be academic-type knowledge (recurrent neural networks are good for text processing) or real-world knowledge (a voice-of-the-customer system typically takes 9 months to implement, start to finish). It is important to understand which types of knowledge any given consultant or firm is bringing to the table: each has its place in the overall project planning process.

Companies that don't involve some kind of project-level AI expertise early on run the risk of going down the wrong path. They might—for instance—decide to develop their own sentiment analysis model, not realizing that in order to build the kind they have in mind they may need a well-tagged dataset of 100,000 call logs (whereas an existing model might get them 80% of what they want with no proprietary training data requirement).

Of course, as with all kinds of outside expertise, you must be careful in evaluating the capabilities of a consultant you are considering hiring. The skills of most consulting firms in the AI domain are still much more marketing than reality. While the knowledge and vocabulary in this book will give you a solid foundation to conduct this type of selection process, you should allot a significant amount of time and resources to the upfront evaluation process to minimize your chances of being led astray by a subpar group.

Product manager

For many organizations, the most important form of non-technical AI expertise will reside at the product manager (or project manager, depending on your company) level. Most companies will not have enough need at the beginning of their AI journey to justify more senior leadership dedicated to AI efforts. Anything lower than product manager risks losing the strategic insight and planning necessary for successful execution of an AI project.

The need for relevant expertise among product managers working on AI projects is similar to the justification for AI-specific consultants: the knowledge can lead to substantially lower implementation costs and much-improved chances of success. Neither an experienced AI technical implementer or a general product manager should be expected to be able to make the most effective tradeoff analysis on critical elements of AI projects: when an out-of-the-box model should be used over a custom-trained one, when an expert system should be developed over a machine learning system, or how much time should be spent on collecting and cleansing training data before focusing the team on model creation. In almost all of these cases, you should expect the ML Engineer or Data Scientist to bias toward more investment in accuracy than is necessary for the business, while the general product manager would underinvest in the foundation needed to achieve the appropriate level of accuracy.

Investment in cultivating AI expertise is probably most underfunded for these types of professionals: non-technical management that can direct the AI development efforts of the organization. Developing these capabilities in-house is critical to correct some of the early missteps in AI implementations that haven't lived up to the hype promised by sensationalist headlines and over-marketed technology solution providers.

Designer

The role of the UI/UX designer in AI-centric software has just begun to be widely explored in the past year or so. The power of AI systems have introduced a new set of design challenges that the general UI/UX designer is ill-equipped to address. For instance, social media companies like Facebook have received a tremendous amount of backlash in converting their news feeds from chronological to AI-driven. While their development has led to higher engagement and (arguably) a more relevant experience for their users, the users themselves become frustrated when they miss content that they would have been exposed to without the curation.

These AI-driven design challenges are virtually brand new in the grand scheme of things and have not yet filtered into any of the common education or training in the design world. You should not expect that most designers will have the tools to be able to address them. There is—however—a small subset of designers who come from AI-centric organizations (like Google or Amazon) who have the experience necessary to know how to address at least some of these problems. There is also a small set of designers who have cultivated a passion for identifying these types of problems whenever they crop up and exploring various potential solutions.

Chapter 9

Areas of Disruption - Near-Term

One of the biggest misconceptions about the field of AI is that it's only the technology of the *future*. People talk about the advent of AI in 10 years, 20 years, 100 years. And while the potential on those time horizons is enormous, that perspective misses the point: artificial intelligence is already here, disrupting the world around us.

Part of the reason that people are unaware of the ubiquity of AI around them was mentioned in the first chapter of this book: one definition of AI is that which hasn't yet been invented. The corollary is that once invented, people no longer consider a technology to be AI. The modern world is rife with examples of intelligent software that would have amazed the people of past decades; and yet, for the most part we take it for granted that these technologies are a part of our lives.

Many of the use cases laid out in previous chapters exemplify such technologies that have reshaped our lives: search engines, targeted advertising, securities trading, recommendation engines, language translation, mail sorting. The list goes on. Work in all of these fields is ongoing and will undoubtedly continue to advance the resulting capabilities of those systems.

This chapter explores the use cases of AI that have not *yet* changed our lives, but are on the verge of doing so. In all of these cases, the enabling technologies have already been invented. In most, there are already examples of companies—both major and startup—exploring how to make the technologies commercially viable.

Customer service

Of all the areas poised for substantial disruption by AI, few strike an emotional nerve with people like customer service. Admittedly, the history of customer service automation is checkered, at best. Cludgy IVRs and chatbots have caused more than a few loyal customers to give up on brands in frustration and disgust. The early disappointment of these systems has led to widespread dismissal of the potential for AI to *ever* do this job well (at least on any timeframe worth discussing).

As with most AI technologies, however, progress on customer service systems has been continuous and steady. The recent surge in AI development over the past few years has allowed systems focused on customer service to advance substantially. Early signs show that such systems will soon be prepared for a much more primary role in companies' customer service options.

Technology

Today, customer service automation primarily shows up in the form of either an IVR (Interactive Voice Response) system on a phone line or a chatbot for web chat. Companies have been implementing basic forms of these systems for decades. For each of these types, development of more advanced systems has been hampered by limitations in enabling technologies. For IVRs, voice-to-text systems historically haven't been good enough for more than a limited set of basic command recognition. For chatbots, the issue has been the inability of AI to understand the complexity of language people use when unconstrained by some kind of menu system.

Voice-to-text technologies have advanced to near-human levels over the past few years. These advancements haven't yet cascaded to commercial applications, but there is nothing fundamental preventing them from doing so in the coming months and years. Implementation of this more advanced technology will allow for much wider adoption of more sophisticated IVR systems.

While general Natural Language Understanding has also advanced substantially, it is still nowhere near human levels of accuracy. For the near-term, chatbots will still need to be constrained in how they allow users to interact with them. However, the advancements that have been made can be combined with a better understanding of *how* it makes sense to constrain these interactions. Over just the past few years, companies have invested tens of millions of dollars in understanding this exact problem better. While there's a substantial element of disappointment that these investments didn't pay off more immediately, they are driving steady progress toward a more automated and satisfying user experience.

Timeline

I estimate that with today's technology, companies could effectively automate about 30% of their customer service. The only thing preventing them from doing so is the rapid rate at which the technology is advancing and the requisite knowledge to make use of it. That deficit is only temporary and is already being addressed.

In the immediate term, the industry will likely see a pull-back of efforts to automate customer service with chatbots due to NLU capabilities not currently matching uninformed expectations. We will, however, see meaningful increase in adoption of IVRs over the next 12-24 months as the voice-to-text advancements cascade.

It will likely be about 5 years before automation of customer service reaches its tipping point. It will take that long for technology advancements to saturate commercial applications and for consumer sentiment of automated systems to inflect. At that point, the automation potential will be closer to 50% due to further advancements in NLU.

10 years out, automation will be the default approach for customer service for almost all businesses. Human agents will be reserved for only the most complex or rare needs (or as a

strategic differentiator for companies that market themselves on service).

Impact

Despite the early struggles of automated customer service systems, I am optimistic that in the near- to medium-term we will see an *improvement* in customer service quality from AI. If AI systems can be implemented more cost effectively than human agents, then it stands to reason that the wait times to be helped will be reduced drastically (theoretically, to nothing).

It is also worth noting that preferences for human interaction are evolving. More and more people would rather not have to interact with a person for transactional matters like checking their account balance or requesting a refund. Satisfying this preference will achieve some (local) societal good. There is an argument that reducing such transactional interaction will lead to *more* authentic human interaction in other domains, though the exploration of that argument falls outside the scope of this section.

It is reasonable to expect that the automation of customer service will lead to a substantial level of cost savings for the companies providing those services. This impact is meaningful: while good industry-level statistics are hard to come by, the annual cost burden of providing contact center services is likely in the tens of billions of dollars.

The flip side of these cost savings is the jobs that they represent. There are roughly 3 million people working in the contact center industry in just the United States, with more world-wide (though, contrary to popular belief, most of the US company workers are actually in the US). These workers form a substantial segment of the labor pool. The loss of these jobs will mean a blow to the economy and a lot of individual distress.

Unfortunately, there is no clear at-scale replacement work for those displaced by customer service automation. Customer service is typically a low-qualification job with only modestly transferable skills. It is not enough to point to previous instances of job displacement that have "worked out fine". For instance, when cars replaced the horses used by stagecoach drivers, the drivers had a clear replacement job driving the new vehicles. There is no such clear alternative for customer service agents.

There is some consolation in that customer service is not—on the whole—particularly desirable work. Employee satisfaction in contact centers is fairly low and churn is notoriously high (average job duration is well under 2 years). Still, it is work that provides financial stability for a massive number of people and we should be thinking more proactively about how to minimize negative impact due to automation in this domain.

Autonomous vehicles

There may be no use case of AI poised to have more impact in the next decade than autonomous vehicles (or "driverless cars"). Autonomous vehicles are one of the rare instances of AI surpassing general expectations: the path to commercial driverless cars that emerged over the last decade caught pretty much everyone by surprise.

The impending release of commercial autonomous vehicles has captured the public's attention, and for good reason: cars are a major lynchpin of our economy and our society. The option to remove a human driver from the equation will have massive impact, most of which we can't even imagine yet.

Technology

Researchers have been exploring the possibility of automating vehicles for decades. In many ways, robotics and driverless technology are one in the same, meaning that the pursuit of autonomous vehicles has been around as long as the field of robotics. The major inflection point in these efforts was around 2007, with the DARPA Urban Grand Challenge. While the vehicles navigating the cityscape in the challenge were not impressive by human standards, their capabilities surprised many observers and fueled increased efforts to make driverless technology a reality.

Autonomous vehicles are a substantially more complex technology than most discussed in this book. They rely on the collaboration of numerous subsystems, each with their own unique development challenges.

Until recent years, the bottleneck for autonomous technology was computer vision. In fact, most historical attempts to automate vehicles did not rely on cameras, as the technology simply wasn't capable of making a video feed a useful input. Those alternative sensing technologies (like radar and LIDAR) are still prevalent across autonomous vehicles today, though traditional cameras have become far more common.

Today's computer vision systems are advanced enough to allow autonomous vehicle operation in the vast majority of conditions (90%+). They are, however, still worse than humans at understanding the environment in poor conditions: heavy precipitation, low light, bad marking or signage. These conditions are the focus of the plurality of the work required to make commercial driverless cars a reality.

The control of autonomous vehicles is a non-trivial problem in its own right. Historically, attempts to manage the steering, braking, and acceleration have relied on manually defining complex sets of rules meant to replicate the behavior of humans. Some modern attempts, however, utilize a more "pure" AI approach to leave the controls to the "judgment" of a set of algorithms. Over time, it is likely that some hybrid of these two approaches proves optimal. For the most part, these systems are already advanced enough for road usage and are not holding up the release of the first autonomous vehicles.

The bulk of navigation is a solved problem thanks to the popularity of GPS guidance systems. However, the edge cases prove to be a remarkably pernicious problem to reach acceptable levels for commercial release. Many of these edge cases reside at the endpoints of a journey: how to get out of the driveway or find a parking spot. Special cases of these problems include areas not found on maps or GPS as well as how to deal with road closures. For many implementations of autonomous vehicle technology, this navigation "long-tail" problem is the constraining factor preventing commercial release today.

There is substantial attention on a higher level "decision-making" intelligence for autonomous vehicles. This is the type of software that would deal with issues like when and why to speed or the infamous "trolley problem" (making decisions on what it means to minimize negative impact in bad situations). While these efforts aren't a blocker to release of autonomous technology, they will play a central role in how the public perceives and adopts the technology, as well as how governments regulate it.

Timeline

Several major automotive manufacturers have targeted the release of their first commercial driverless car before the end of 2020 (about a year from time of writing). Although this timeline is astonishing to many, it does seem feasible. In many ways, a fully autonomous vehicle is just an extension of technologies that are already on the road today: smart lane keeping, autonomous parking, collision avoidance systems. Prototype systems have been on the road for years and have clocked millions of miles.

It is worth noting that while we will likely see fully autonomous cars in the next few years, they will *not* be autonomous all the time. The long-tail problems mentioned above will plague the technology for years to come. Human intervention will still be required in poor visibility conditions or when some kind of complicated judgment is required. However, we can expect even these early cars to take over the vast majority of driving activity.

Projections for adoption of autonomous vehicles vary widely. My own personal projections for the US fall along the lines of:

- 2020: First commercial autonomous vehicle
- 2025: 10% of vehicles on the road
- 2030: 25% of vehicles on the road
- 2040: 50% of vehicles on the road
- 2050: 75% of vehicles and first serious proposals of banning non-autonomous vehicles nationwide

Impact

It is almost impossible to overestimate the impact that autonomous vehicles will have, even in the medium term. Part of that comes from my optimism in the above projections: very few casual observers would guess that they would see the outlawing of human drivers in their lifetime. But even if the adoption curve is much slower than the above projection, driverless cars are going to have much more impact than most people expect.

Although estimates vary somewhat, there are approximately 5 million people employed to drive a vehicle in the United States. Many of these are hybrid roles that perform tasks other than driving (like mail delivery) that can't be automated away by a driverless car; however, if the driving portion can be automated, many of these jobs will likely see a structural change that shifts the human worker's focus away from that aspect of the job.

The impact on employment is potentially even more serious than it is for customer service, as it could affect even more jobs. The lack of transferable skills that would allow displaced workers to find alternative vocations is even more troublesome for professional drivers. The one silver lining is that professional driving jobs are even less desirable than customer service: the stress, boredom, and health risks lead to substantial turnover in the industry. In fact, there is a decade-long labor shortage of professional drivers that is expected to get worse before autonomous vehicle technology is adopted.

The flipside of the employment impact is substantial cost savings for companies spanning almost the entire economy. Over-the-road delivery is an $800B industry in the United States, with nearly half the cost-base attributable to drivers' wages. The adoption of autonomous technology will eventually cut an enormous amount of cost out of the economy, ultimately leading to significant savings for consumers and allowing for a complete restructuring of how we think about supply chains.

As large as the economic impact of driverless cars will be, it may be dwarfed by the technology's other impacts on society. The rest of this section will attempt to describe some of those potential impacts. However, the reality may be even more significant than described here; it is easy to take for granted just how tightly coupled our modern world is to the fact that humans have to drive cars.

One of the better predictors of adult happiness is the length of their commute. Long commutes take up a substantial portion of people's lives, have almost no intrinsic reward, and can greatly contribute to stress. Eliminating the need for people to pay attention while in the car may also eliminate the negative impact that commuting has on happiness.

The freedom that driving grants is restricted from certain individuals. Many kinds of physical (and mental) disabilities prevent people from being able to legally operate a vehicle. Those limitations will be quickly overcome if the person does not need to operate the vehicle, granting a level of personal freedom that has never before been known in history. This impact will also be felt by children who would otherwise be too young to drive, though the extent to which they are allowed unsupervised access to this freedom is not yet clear (from a legal, societal, or familial standpoint).

The metropolitan city structure that dominates much of American culture is largely based on the time, attention, and energy costs associated with driving long distances (this is very tied to the previous commuting point). As those costs decrease with autonomous technology, it is likely that we see a reshaping of city structure, with the geographic limits of suburbs expanding. The implications of this restructuring are very difficult to predict.

The tight coupling of commercial buildings with adjacent parking will be eliminated. Parking lots (and especially parking decks) will become less common. When they do exist, they will be in areas with lower real estate costs.

Car ownership will be transformed. As cars will be able to drive themselves to where they are needed, a new model of car sharing (basically a much-scaled-up version of ride sharing) will emerge. The total number of cars built and owned may drop by as much as 90%.

As cars develop the ability to drive themselves through the night without an attentive driver, the usefulness of road-side hotels and motels will be almost entirely eliminated. This could lead to the collapse of that industry. Other forms of long-distance transportation (e.g., air travel) will likely also see a substantial negative impact, though probably not to the same degree.

The reduction in short-distance delivery costs (e.g., for dinner) will greatly increase the prevalence of delivery behavior. Dining out and at-home cooking will likely both see significant decreases.

Media generation

Unlike autonomous vehicles, the potential for AI to generate media from scratch had gotten virtually zero attention from the broad public before 2019. And while driving is undoubtedly a cornerstone of our society and economy, you could argue that media consumption is an even *more* important element.

The lack of awareness is partially due to the novelty of the technology. GANs (the enabling technology) were just invented in 2014 and didn't gain popularity even among the technical community until 2017 or so. In comparison with the decades that researchers have been working on autonomous vehicles, AI media generation is just too new for people to know much about it.

However, the lack of awareness on this topic is unacceptable. And—fortunately—the news media is beginning to pick up on the subject and feature it to spread awareness. And for good reason: while the economic impacts of automated media generation are meaningful, the societal impacts are potentially so large as to be hard to fathom. Much of the trust in our society is predicated on the assumption that you can trust what you see and hear. If you see a video of someone clearly committing a crime, you can be fairly confident that the person committed the crime. The implication of AI media generation is that *we can no longer have that trust.*

Technology

AI media generation is largely the domain of Generative Adversarial Networks (GANs), a new type of deep learning model that is built for creating images or sound. While exploration of their potential is very much ongoing, so far GANs (as well as a few other deep learning models) have been demonstrated to be able to:

- Generate human-level speech audio for any given text
- Mimic the voice and speaking style of any given person (though this has not yet been publicly demonstrated in conjunction with human-level speech generation)
- Edit video to adjust a person's facial expressions and lip movements with quality that is convincing on casual viewing
- Reconstruct partially obscured areas of an image
- Transpose the artistic style of one image to another
- Create realistic-looking basic objects (flowers, birds) in low resolution images based on a description

Today, there are virtually no implementations of these technologies in software that is publicly accessible and usable. What does exist requires a significant degree of technical acumen to make use of. However, as the commercial uses of the technology mature, the tools available for general use will proliferate. Companies like Adobe have already made clear their plans for integrating the technology into their software offerings.

Timeline

Because the types of models used to generate media are so new, it is not clear how quickly the technology will advance to the point that it can cost-effectively create media suitable for consumption by the general public. Progress has been so rapid over the past few years that I would not be surprised to see the emergence of fraudulent sound and video clips masquerading as authentic within the next 24 months.

It's possible that we will see the emergence of AI generated media used for political attacks for the 2020 presidential election. I would be surprised if it's not a meaningful problem by the 2024 election.

Projecting out further than the next decade on such a young technology is mostly an exercise in futility, but I would be surprised if the CGI industry as it exists today isn't completely reshaped by this technology in my lifetime.

Impact

The economic impact that AI-generated media may have on the computer graphics (CGI) industry is not inconsequential. The industry accounts for billions of dollars of the economy and much of it is vulnerable to disruption. Also, the reduction in computer graphics cost could unlock more prolific and rich stories that rely on the graphics. However, that impact is small in comparison with the potential negative impact on society of making fraudulent media easy to create.

Because it is generally not cost-effectively possible to falsify, video (and audio, to a lesser extent) is considered to be good evidence. This is true in the legal system, in public perception, and in private matters.

If the technical progress of media generation outstrips public awareness, there's potential for serious societal cost if bad actors make accusations and observers don't know to question the authenticity of the evidence presented. With any luck, this period of time can be shortened or even eliminated by maximizing awareness of the potential issues as much as possible.

After awareness of the issue spreads, the more pernicious issue will be one of trust. It is highly unlikely that society abandons video and audio as evidence entirely. Instead, we will need new processes and tools for determining the likelihood of authenticity of any given piece of evidence.

Unfortunately, technological approaches to authenticity verification are unlikely to have long-term potential. The nature of the generative algorithms is such that any advancements in fraud detection can be incorporated to improve the quality of the fraud over time. Still, it is possible to imagine a "white hat" vs. "black hat" technology race, similar to how the cybersecurity industry works.

For public figures, some form of tracking will likely become necessary. For high profile events this is not an issue: there are enough people in attendance to generally validate or refute most claims. However, many public figures will likely also want some form of protection covering their time when they aren't in the spotlight. It is difficult to envision what the specifics of such a system might look like, but the implications of any form of tracking are very serious in terms of privacy trade-offs.

If AI media generation becomes easy enough to use, it is not difficult to imagine it playing a role in the more private affairs of everyday people. Video and audio can be used as evidence of illegal activity, infidelity, and any number of other serious allegations that can have deep ramifications for someone's life. The defense against these "weapons" is not immediately clear for people outside the public spotlight. Even in a book full of high potential technologies, this is a fact that should give you pause.

Automated employee compliance tracking

In the near future, it will become far more common for employers to have software systems that automatically monitor the activities of their employees to prevent undesired behavior. This use case is interesting because it is one that society has been anticipating—and fearing—for decades, yet now that it's here, it's getting relatively little attention.

Technology

The major impediment to companies tracking their employees' behavior more closely for compliance purposes has been the resources required to do so. Manual review of these activities in detail is impossible: you would need twice as many employees (not to mention the question of who monitors the monitors). Companies have looked for ways to automate this process for decades and have implemented limited systems to do so in areas with little sophistication that are easy to monitor.

With the increasing capability of machine learning to process unstructured data, companies' desire to monitor their employees' detailed activity is becoming more of a reality. NLP can detect keywords from email that might indicate an employee is trying to defraud the company. Voice-to-text can be layered on to ensure that registered financial advisors are not inappropriately promising returns to their clients.

Much of this technology now exists and has begun to mature over the past few years. The only remaining steps for ubiquity are employer awareness of the possibilities and additional sophistication of the NLP technology to detect more complex forms of non-compliance.

Timeline

The fraud and financial advisor applications that I mentioned previously already exist commercially today. There are dozens of similar use cases that are now feasible and being experimented with. The main constraint to more rapid adoption is just general awareness and a better understanding of where investment in monitoring systems is best spent.

Adoption of compliance tracking will likely be largely driven by non-compliance events. Infamous examples like Wells Fargo's employees opening up fake accounts in customers' names and Equifax losing massive amounts of their customers' sensitive personal data lead to substantial investment of time and money by employers to implement new processes in an attempt to prevent similar events from occurring. These periods of investment will result more and more in the implementation of AI-driven employee monitoring systems.

While it is difficult to predict how quickly companies will adopt compliance tracking systems in response to negative events, it seems probable that the majority of major corporations will have some form of tracking implemented within the next 10 years.

Impact

There will be substantial improvements to the overall economy from more prolific automated monitoring of employee behavior. If this technology can prevent the types of costs that consumers bear today for issues like what happened with Wells Fargo and Equifax, then there is a clear argument for the implementation cost of the systems (at least from this one dimension). Substantial benefits can be gained both in terms of pure monetary savings as well as less tangible consumer happiness.

The (very serious) tradeoff is the privacy of the employees being monitored. While the right of employers to monitor their workers is well-known and generally not an issue, the main constraint to companies *exercising* that right is the cost of doing so. As the cost comes down and oversight increases in lock-step, there will be significant concerns.

For the most part, detailed employee surveillance is only kicked off today in response to some kind of incident. This post-facto paradigm minimizes false positives: if you already know there's an issue, then you're looking for the evidence to explain what happened. In a surveillance-first environment, the rate of false positives will go up substantially. Companies will flag employee behavior that has likely always been happening (with no tangible detriment) and seek to correct it (arguably unnecessarily). While it is the company's legal right to take this action, that doesn't necessarily mean that it maximizes societal (or even business) good.

This looming issue gives rise to a major question around what is appropriate for companies to monitor. While illegal activity is clearly within the purview of monitoring, should the company have a formal policy preventing discussion of off-work activities that it finds inappropriate? If an employee is discussing drinking and party plans for the next weekend with a coworker friend, what is the company's role in monitoring and preventing that conversation?

While the privacy concern of employee monitoring may not delve as deep into the core of our society as our trust in video evidence, it is fundamental nevertheless. Loss of privacy can result in all kinds of undesirable outcomes, as has been explored by stories like *1984* and in repressive political regimes.

Government surveillance

Automated surveillance by government entities is the big—and far more sinister—brother of employee tracking by corporations. Science fiction writers have warned of the omniscient police state for decades. Once the technology exists, there is nothing stopping well-intentioned (or not) governments from closely monitoring their citizens' every movement to enforce order—or so the argument goes.

While it may be tempting to write off the concerns of Orwell and Vonnegut as hyperbole, as a society we are now closer than ever to the subjects of those concerns becoming a reality. Each passing year, the potential for the use of AI by governments for incredibly detailed person-level tracking becomes more and more real.

The scary thing about the use of AI for government surveillance is that none of the individual steps toward dystopia look that unreasonable. Police have used video footage as evidence for as long as video has existed; why not automate the identification of people in video? Social media feeds often have evidence of criminal activity; why not identify that activity with software instead of putting someone in front of a computer screen searching for it?

The seeming reasonableness of developing AI for surveillance means that our society's march toward that future seems inexorable. The fact that surveillance may be the path of least resistance means that applications of AI in service of that goal are some of the most dangerous and warrant some of the most careful review.

Technology

Government surveillance is one area where the available technology already far outstrips the implemented applications. Facial recognition software is already nearly perfected. This software was a natural extension of the object detection work with convnets that sparked the current AI revolution. With a little adaptation, faces proved to be a far simpler domain than arbitrary objects and companies like Google and Facebook achieved superhuman performance in the past few years.

In the past 18 months, China has assumed the mantle of technical and commercial superiority for facial recognition AI. In fact, this is one of the few specific applications where the fears around China's rise in the AI field are well-founded. Investors and the government have poured hundreds of millions of dollars into funding the adaptation of academic algorithms into software tools ready to be used by police forces.

Algorithms for identifying signals in social media were pioneered over the past decade by the field of marketing automation. The idea was that software could identify the small tells that a person might be predisposed to buy your product with accuracy greater than a human and at a much larger scale. While this type of automation has seen only modest success in the broader field of marketing, the technology showed a great deal of promise for police forces (and tech companies hoping to earn their contracts).

Today, numerous companies like Palantir and Dataminr ingest every bit of publicly available information they can find in the hopes of identifying these signals. They search for keywords and phrases like "I'm going to kill…" and even use photo object recognition (to look for firearms, for instance). Their insights have earned them hundreds of millions of dollars in contracts with governments and security forces all over the world.

Timeline

The technologies mentioned in the previous section are being applied at-scale today. In early April Singapore put out its first proposal for a city-wide connected camera network with integrated facial recognition. Around the same time China piloted a new police headset with built-in facial recognition tied to a database of arrest warrants; they arrested over 30 people in a single day by standing in the middle of a busy train station.

Disturbing as it is to say, the application of advanced AI to surveillance today is only being limited by imagination. Given the resources at the disposal of the countless enforcement authorities around the world, it is likely that a surge in the development of such technologies will occur as soon as news of the positive results of the first successful trials spreads.

It is worth noting that some of the more advanced technologies pictured in fictional works aren't quite a reality today. The ever-present "enhance" functionality for videos and images doesn't yet exist (though GANs are being developed that will attempt just this). To the best of my knowledge, there is no AI today that can accurately recognize the "gait" of a person in a video or identify them based on their iris from 100 feet away.

But I have seen research in these directions and don't have much optimism that these very technologies are over a decade away.

Impact

The development of AI surveillance will be driven by the demand for more effective and less costly ways to administer justice: preventing crimes before they happen and tracking down those that perpetrate them afterward. It is doubtless that AI will prove a useful tool for both of these objectives.

It's outside the scope of this book to explore the myriad ways in which automated governmental surveillance could be a disaster. There is no shortage of books treating that topic in depth. If you don't buy what they're selling, it's unlikely I'll convince you differently here.

As the use of technology by police increases, it is important as a society that we continue to push for our rights of due process and privacy. It is also important to stay vigilant against the indirect approaches to enabling an AI-first surveillance state. One of these approaches is granting open access to data. The oversteps of the NSA and the government at large should be very concerning in the context of security forces that can process massive amounts of information automatically.

Human-computer interface

One of the less-heralded impending AI-driven transformations is how humans interact with computers. Voice interfaces and chat interfaces have now hit the mainstream, but the adoption we're seeing so far is just the tip of the iceberg. Since the advent of computing, humans' ability to interact with their machines has mostly been limited to the mouse and keyboard (ignoring the interfaces at the beginning of computing before the invention of the mouse) in a highly constrained environment. Over the past decade, touch (and touch keyboard) have also arisen—in an even more constrained setting. Those limitations are quickly being eliminated and it is difficult to guess exactly how our interface technology will adjust.

The most logical expansion of computer control is in the realm of natural language. In fact, much early human-computer interface (HCI) relied on natural language input through the keyboard. This paradigm dominated before the invention of the GUI, through the command-line interface. It was also manifested in early computer games called "text adventures", where the player would type out the actions they wanted to take. Now that AI has made understanding natural language easier, we will almost certainly see a proliferation of these interfaces (ala Siri, Alexa, and any one of the thousands of chatbots that have popped up in the past few years).

Beyond language, it is also reasonable to believe that we will see an increase in control systems developed around video technology. The iPhone X face unlock functionality is a small taste of the possibility in that realm. It is not much of a stretch to believe that more systems will harness gesture recognition, facial expression recognition, and eye tracking technologies to make certain aspects of computing easier.

Although the technology is still nascent, it is possible that direct thought detection will arise as a powerful HCI methodology in the medium term. This is the dream for sci-fi computer designers: removing the hardware in the middle and allowing a person to communicate directly with a digital system using just their brain.

Technology

The voice-to-text capabilities of today's AI systems are already advanced enough to unlock much of the potential of voice-control systems. These applications are being actively explored by all of the major tech giants with systems that have become widely recognized, like Siri and Alexa.

The NLP capabilities backing voice-control and chatbots have advanced significantly over the past few years, but they're still far from matching human-level understanding. The development of natural language based control systems will occur in lock-step with the underlying NLP technology. I believe that the potential of today's underlying technology has not been fully realized by any modern control system, but there is significant investment across the industry to identify more powerful and natural systems.

The computer vision technology necessary to power camera-based control mostly exists today. The number of projects seeking to adapt this technology to commercial applications is fairly limited, however. The constraint for commercial adoption of these new control models is mostly based on general awareness and the creativity of those applying the technology.

As opposed to the other control technologies, direct thought detection (sometimes called Brain-Computer Interface, or BCI) is still very early. The potential of the technology has been demonstrated in limited settings, but there are virtually no commercial applications today. What does exist in the real world is mostly experimental treatment for various forms of neurological impairments.

There is some cause for optimism around the adoption of BCI technology in the medium-term. In the past few years there has been substantial venture capital investment in startups seeking to develop non-invasive brain wave detectors, such as MindMaze. If these technologies are ultimately not able to achieve the reaction time or signal clarity required for control applications, there is also some investment in more invasive technologies that require implanting of a device in the user's brain. The most famous of these is Elon Musk's Neuralink.

Timeline

Adoption of voice and natural language control systems has been increasing for decades. The recent surge in smart home devices (particularly Amazon Echo and Google Home) has greatly contributed to the commonality of these types of systems in the average consumer's life. While broader adoption of the technologies across society is difficult to measure or predict, it seems safe to say that it will become far more common than it is today over the course of the next 10 to 20 years.

Widespread adoption of camera-based control depends on the development of a compelling application for its use. Room-scale virtual reality is one such application, though widespread adoption of VR is a large question on its own. It is likely that niche uses for camera-based control will find adoption in the next 5 years. It is less clear if the paradigm will ever find the right uses to become dominant in comparison to other types of control.

The timeline around BCI is very much undetermined. It is possible that non-invasive technology like MindMaze's will find limited applications within the next 5 to 10 years. Given the state of the art of that type of technology, it seems unlikely that it offers the performance necessary to become a dominant control methodology. Implanted device-based control offers much more promise, but also has a significantly longer timeline. Elon Musk has famously estimated compelling commercial uses of the Neuralink technology within a decade, but many expert observers believe at least 20 years is a more reasonable horizon.

Impact

The evolution of HCI will allow for far deeper integration of computing into our lives. The impact could be as significant as the development of the GUI: widening the accessibility of computers from programmers to the mass public. Most parents can look to tablets and smartphones for a glimpse of the possibilities: many young children learn to navigate such devices long before they learn to talk. Removing the need for a screen and limited touch-, mouse-, or keyboard-based inputs should effect even greater change.

Most of the real-world uses of evolved HCI technologies are still far from the light of day, and therefore difficult to imagine. However, they will emerge over the coming years. Possibilities include asking your shopping cart for directions in the grocery store, telling your computer to buy you movie tickets (and expecting it to work!), flipping the pages of an ebook with just your eyes, and opening doors with a wave of your hand.

Most of the impact from this technology is likely around marginal improvements in quality of life. After all, we've done pretty well to-date getting computers to do what we want with a mouse and keyboard. This technology is likely more about convenience than fundamental transformation, as opposed to some of the other technologies discussed in this chapter.

The exception to this marginal improvement is for those with physical disabilities. The ability to control the computer without the use of your hands is enormous for a quadriplegic.

The possibility of having a conversation with a smart device means a lot to someone who can't see. While these cases may account for a small portion of the overall population, the improvements in their ability to use computers will be incredibly meaningful.

Chapter 10

Areas of Disruption - Long-Term

While there is tremendous potential for the application of existing AI technologies to novel use cases, the disruption in these areas we'll see in coming years pales in comparison to the long-term impact we'll see from technologies that are yet to be invented.

A word of warning: I am among those who believe that AI will reshape our society fundamentally, even within the next generation or two. Given the rate of development of AI technologies, making predictions about anything beyond a few years out is a risky proposition. Still, based on how I've seen AI affect our world in just the past few years, it's hard for me to believe that society will continue in its current state.

It's worth noting that the long-term impacts of AI on society are a topic of much debate. In fact, most researchers at the forefront of AI research believe that AI's impact will be far more gradual and incremental. I personally think they've been conditioned to that line of reasoning by previous AI winters, but also recognize that they have more technical authority on the topic than I do. Who you choose to believe is a matter of your own judgment.

Physical labor

In some ways, the automation of physical labor has been the ultimate goal of technological progress for centuries. And AI has played a significant role in the early stages of the satisfaction of that goal: robots now play a major role in the factories of all developed nations. One of the most startlingly underreported stories of the AI renaissance is how it was presaged in the manufacturing sector. Since 2000, U.S. manufacturing output has increased by 24% while the human labor employed has decreased by 29%. We're in the middle of a collapse of the factory labor market and very few people seem to realize it.

Indeed, when people talk about the collapse of America's manufacturing power, they're really just talking about employment rates. The actual output of the U.S. manufacturing industry has increased at a relatively steady rate since at least the middle of the 20th century. The key that commentators miss is robotics (or AI).

There is no sign that the trend of automation in manufacturing is going to abate any time soon. In some ways, it closely mirrors the automation (or optimization) of the agriculture industry, which accounted for around 90% of U.S. jobs in the 18th century, but makes up less than 2% now. While we still may be decades away from an outcome that drastic for the industrial sector, there is little reason to believe that the decline will end at any point before then.

Of course, manufacturing is just a portion of the physical labor performed in our society. Physical labor encompasses cleaning, food prep, electrical and plumbing work, construction, and a host of other jobs. In fact, manual labor still accounts for nearly a third of employment in the United States.

A portion of these jobs are safe for the foreseeable future. Much of plumbing and electrical work rely on the exact type of dynamic problem solving ability that AI is still quite bad at. Cleaning and food prep—however—do not seem to be so safe from automation. Millions of dollars are already pouring into technology companies that hope to disrupt each of these industries. There is no clear winner with a dominant solution yet, but it feels like that kind of breakthrough is just around the corner.

There are three primary problems in the field of robotics that have prevented the majority of the realm of physical labor from beginning the march toward automation that the manufacturing sector has seen: movement in an arbitrary environment designed for humans, manipulating arbitrary objects, and deciding what to do in a dynamic environment. All three of these problems have been the subject of substantial research focus over the past couple of decades. All three have seen remarkable progress, with the first demonstrations of limited human-like capability on at least the first two.

Impact

As mentioned, the automation of manual labor has been a dream of technological progress for far longer than anyone has been alive today. The realization of that dream has many benefits: jobs centered around labor are notoriously exhausting, unfulfilling, and often result in long-term physical health impairment. All else equal, it's the rare individual who would choose to spend a day in back-breaking labor. If physical labor can be automated, it will free up a broad swath of society for more enriching pursuits.

For the broader economy, automation means a substantial reduction in the cost of performing labor. All industries tied to the collection, processing, and distribution of physical goods (which is almost all of them) will see benefits. The cost of goods for the end consumer will drop over time. Assuming the robots we develop are able to process the resources required for their own manufacture, we may see the first glimpse of the feedback loop required for society to enter an era without scarcity.

It is hard to overstate the potential positive benefit of labor automation. Still, it is somewhat outside the scope of this book to give that potential future a thorough treatment.

On the flip side, there may be substantial societal costs during the transition period of labor automation. As mentioned, even in the developed world a substantial portion of the population relies on wages earned from physical labor. As those tasks are automated, it is not clear where a physical skill set might best be applied for direct economic gain.

Many would argue that the societies of the past (and present) have weathered previous upheavals of economic order with relatively little society-level cost. The transition in the U.S. from an agrarian economy to an industrial one is a prime example. The replacement of horses with automobiles is another, though on a much smaller scale.

I resist pacification in the face of these arguments for two reasons: previous shifts happened over a much longer time frame and had a much more obvious replacement job.

On the subject of timeframe: the transition from agrarian to industrial economy happened over the span of centuries. This makes sense in the pre-information age, where the secrets of efficient manufacturing were passed on by individual experts. It's unlikely that the effects of software progress will be similarly hindered. I believe that we'll face an employment crisis over the course of a few decades, not centuries.

As far as replacement work goes, it's not hard to see how a farmer accustomed to hard labor in their fields might adapt to a similar physical rigor within the walls of a plant. Although the cognitive demands of manufacturing certainly outstrip those of farming, much of that load is borne by management; most of the line workers need only a modest amount of training before becoming an effective component of the process.

When manual labor is automated entirely, it is not clear what the natural replacement work is. While optimists are spot on that there will be new opportunities in the knowledge economy as a result of the rise of AI, it is unclear that those opportunities will be practical for the large portion of the population displaced from their physical roles.

If—as the pessimists predict—unemployment is the natural outcome for those displaced from jobs centered on physical labor, then our society may be in for a challenge that it has never faced before. Even during the Great Depression, the unemployment rate never got much past 20%. How much worse will it be if that rate exceeds 30% with no clear natural resolution?

Software development

Even among those who are worried about the outcomes of mass-automation from AI, common logic holds that it's only *routine* work that will be automated in the foreseeable future. And indeed, repetitive tasks that rely on basic pattern matching or rule-following are the most likely candidates for early automation.

However, as AI steadily grows more advanced, it's likely that our definition of "routine" tasks will edge more and more to the complex. Computer progress on board games offers an interesting parallel: it wasn't so many years ago that no one believed AI would outperform humans at the game of chess. When Deep Blue did achieve supremacy, there was a substantial amount of retroactive justification. Rather than a showcase of human ingenuity, chess was redefined as a relatively simple set of possible moves and outcomes: the perfect type of problem for a "brute force" solution from a dumb computer.

We're already seeing a similar redefinition with the game of Go. Similar to the chess example, many experts believed AI was still a decade away from professional-level Go play right up until AlphaGo defeated Lee Sedol. Now that there are several superhuman Go players, pessimists are using the exact same logic that was used to belittle the Deep Blue accomplishment. They say that Go has a fixed set of possible moves and that the computer's superiority doesn't require creativity or abstract problem solving. There is also a significant line of criticism that AlphaGo can beat top Go players, but can't even play tic-tac-toe (for the most part, that argument was roundly disproven with the advent of AlphaZero, which now sits atop the chess rankings as well as Go).

The failure of both experts and society to accurately predict AI's success in gaming—as well as their reactions after the fact—offer an interesting lesson for predictions of future AI superhuman achievements. Namely: we (as a society) are bad at determining the types of problems AI will excel at ahead of time, consistently fail to accurately predict AI's progress on cognitive tasks, and have a blinding hubris on those tasks that we consider to be *particularly* indicative of our species' cognitive superiority.

In the previous chapter, I laid out several areas of cognitive work that face near-term pressure from AI: legal work, finance, customer service. It's hard to think of a job that *doesn't* have the potential to be at least partially automated over the next decade or so. But there's one type of work that is particularly interesting to examine.

One of the potential "hopes" for humanity's continued productivity in an automated world is that new demands for talent will be created. If systems are taking over physical labor or routine cognitive tasks, then it seems reasonable that those systems must be *created*. And for now, that type of creation is well outside the capabilities of even advanced AI systems. So— some say—you don't need to worry about employment opportunities, you just need to skill up to satisfy the new demands for labor that will be created.

In an AI-first world, it seems reasonable that the new demands for talent will be focused around software creation (programming). And it is true that programming has resisted automation up until now. While developer tools are constantly being released that make programmers more efficient, vanishingly few of those tools do the work *for* the programmer.

However, beyond wishful thinking, there's little reason to believe that there's anything inherent in software development that prevents it from the automation potential of AI. This idea is difficult for some: if AI can program, then it's not much of a jump for it to improve itself. And that sets off a feedback loop with some scary implications. Despite that concern (or perhaps because of it), it is important to assess the possibility seriously. In fact, there are several specific areas of programming where investigations into automation have already begun.

Cybersecurity as a whole sees a relatively high degree of automation. Many types of attacks rely on a scale that could never be achieved by manual effort. Likewise, intrusion and vulnerability detection take advantage of the speed and attentiveness of algorithms to achieve broader coverage than even a team of people could on their own. Similarly, software testing has relied on automated test algorithms for years. Admittedly, in both of these fields automation is only a *piece* of the overall picture, with almost all of the complicated problem solving still being done by human professionals. Still, this is how automation works in every field: the simplest tasks are tackled first, then the algorithms progress into steadily more challenging problems.

The beginnings of automation in cybersecurity and testing lay the groundwork for expanded capabilities in other areas of development. There are now several startups (like DeepCode) building systems for automated analysis of code in a variety of different languages, looking for bugs, inefficiencies, and opportunities to apply best practices. The most advanced of these systems learn from the contributions of their highest capability users. It is not too much of a stretch to imagine these systems improving to make more and more proactive recommendations, albeit in an advisory capacity.

Some companies are exploring more advanced methods of developing systems that can adapt to complicated, unforeseeable environments. Viv, a company building a next-gen digital assistant, made a splash in 2016 when it described it's method of evaluating users' queries: making use of a library of elementary code blocks or mini-algorithms that could then be assembled dynamically in response to the query to provide the best solution/answer. Viv was acquired by Samsung later that year and virtually no news of the group's development has surfaced since, but it's likely that other companies are exploring advanced ways for their systems to reassemble themselves as their needs and environments shift.

Of course, there's a long way to go from the basic types of automation we're seeing in programming today to full-blown "no need for human developers anymore". And it is certainly true that there are many types of jobs that are likely to vanish before computer programmers. But it is particularly important to assess the potential for automation in this domain given that it's so often held up as a bastion against the obsolescence of the human worker.

Impact

As mentioned, the automation of programming is likely to be progressive (as opposed to every developer waking up one morning without a job). The current talent shortage in software development will almost certainly continue to get worse before it starts getting better. To that end, in terms of jobs there are relatively few downsides to the automation of software development in the short and medium terms. Automation helping companies solve more problems with code will help society.

As automation does progress, however, it may serve as a sort of bellwether for the broader non-routine cognitive job sector. Programming is among the most complex jobs in terms of abstract problem solving and adaptability to arbitrary contexts. As elements of programming are automated, it's a strong sign that similar progress is likely not far behind in other domains (in fact, that progress has probably already occurred by the time automation reaches software development).

As AI does begin to eat into the overall employment opportunities available for software developers, I believe our society as we know it will reach an inflection point from which we are likely to never return. If AI can obviate the need for human programmers, then it probably isn't all that long until human workers as a whole are superfluous, at least on the scale that drives our economy and society. The scope of the issues this eventuality will create dwarfs the impact of automation in the physical and routine domains. While optimists argue that automation is accompanied by net job creation, it is hard to argue for additional opportunities when the AI is *programming itself*.

Of course, there are substantial societal implications outside of employment. To the extent that AI has the potential to perpetuate societal injustice, the risk is magnified by the prominent role that software will play in an AI-first world. If data and algorithms are at risk of bias, then that risk is almost certainly compounded when algorithms *create* the algorithms. Due to this multiplicative effect, the vigilance of applying AI in an ethical manner is even more important when it comes to the automation of software development.

The ultimate implication of AI taking over software development is that it will also take over *AI development*. AI will begin to program itself, and it will do so at a speed and scope that humans can't match. This creates the possibility of a runaway intelligence scenario, often called the "singularity". Given the exponential rate of technological advancement, AI may begin to cultivate an intelligence that leaves humans in the dust.

The idea of the singularity has been explored extensively in other works. One of the most prominent thinkers in the space is Ray Kurzweil, who wrote *The Singularity is Near*. Even putting aside dedicated literature, it's hard to escape discussion of runaway AI scenarios; they permeate the majority of broad coverage of the field of AI. Significant further exploration of these scenarios lies outside the scope of this book. Just know that the possibility of this outcome is real and that there are many intelligent and informed technologists concerned about its reality (though to be fair, there are also many who discount the risk of this scenario for a number of valid potential reasons).

Resource allocation

One of the hallmarks of advanced intelligent software is the ability to manipulate a set of parameters in order to optimize (maximize or minimize) a given outcome. While this optimization often happens on an individual decision-making basis, the underlying principle is not limited in scope. Just as AI can make a decision on a single applicant's creditworthiness for a loan, it can also make decisions across an entire portfolio of potential investments so as to maximize profit. In fact, when applied at the system-wide level, AI can sometimes be even easier to apply and show greater results, as it has all of the parameters within its control (and therefore doesn't need to accommodate the less predictable behavior of human agents in the system).

For the most part, today's visions of AI fail to grasp the implications of its potential to be applied at scale. This makes sense: automated decision-making is not yet a trusted component of most of our society's systems. Its reliability has to be proven out at the micro level before it can be properly considered for broader applications. However, as time passes, algorithms improve, and we come to trust AI with more responsibility, it is inevitable that more and more consequential and large-scale decisions will be left to software.

This evolution is intuitive: AI is good at handling large amounts of information and distilling out an answer that satisfies the specified constraints. It makes sense that it should ultimately be given responsibility for large and complex systems: global supply chains, assignment of skilled workers to tackle complicated problems, infrastructure planning and development. In short, AI will come to be responsible for much of the resource allocation in our society.

Today, society-level resource allocation is handled by a convoluted mixture of capitalism and bureaucracy. Corporations and our monetary system attempt to ensure some kind of equitable distribution of resources on an individual basis, taking into account the relative contributions of the individual back into society. Where this system fails—or is blatantly unfair—government and nonprofits step in to attempt to cover the difference. The divvying of responsibility for resources among these parties is determined mostly by tradition and the leverage of power or influence.

By nature, today's solutions for distribution of resources are unfair and subjective. Not all contributions to society are measured the same way and not all members of society are capable of contributing in equal measures. Philanthropy is most often allocated according to what makes the philanthropist feel best. Government-controlled resources are deployed to whomever makes the most noise (or more accurately, whomever has the ear of those responsible). None of this is meant as a rejection of our current solutions: they're the best we've come up with after millennia of iteration.

The failures of today's systems offer a clear opportunity for AI. If given a clear set of optimization parameters, an AI system can get much closer to equitable distribution than our current systems. It will be impartial by nature, drawing allocations objectively according to the rules that it's been given. Designed properly, it will be incapable of being bribed or allowing emotion to get in the way of creating the most good.

In theory, such a future system could go a long way in curing the chronic problems of a scarcity-based society: hunger, homelessness, poor access to healthcare, and many others. Viewed at a macro level, most of the resources required are already available. The global economy is more than capable of generating sufficient food, shelter, and basic medical care for everyone on the planet. The challenge is one of allocation and logistics. An AI-run system couldn't solve these problems overnight, but could likely get much closer than the imperfect systems we have today.

Impact

As with many of the major areas that AI stands to disrupt, it's hard to overestimate the potential impact AI will have on resource allocation in the long run. Our world has always struggled with problems like hunger and homelessness. A possible future in which these problems are largely solved sounds more like fantasy than a realistic roadmap for technology.

And yet, there's no reason to believe that this type of world-changing capability is beyond the feasibility of AI. In fact, much of the technology required already exists today (smaller cousins of such systems are already in use for planning deliveries in global networks, directing international air traffic, maintaining industrial fleets with millions of units). The real challenges are likely in agreeing on sets of objectives and parameters for the systems to operate under, then convincing those who hold decision-making authority today to relinquish their control.

To be fair, this utopian vision would require substantial sacrifice to achieve. That's why ideas like socialism and universal basic income meet so much resistance: redistribution of resources means that those who have a lot today must give much of it up. In the short to medium term, it's difficult to imagine our society signing up for that kind of reallocation willingly.

In all likelihood, the impact of AI-controlled resource allocation will first be felt in small pockets where resources are already being controlled and allocated in a central manner. Perhaps funding for a school system at the county level will be distributed to programs according to an intelligent model's understanding of where it will have the most impact (this is already happening in some ways today). Or deployment of international aid workers will be determined by an algorithm where today it would fall on an overworked director.

These small deployments of AI allocation require no sacrifice: they improve outcomes and decrease administrative costs. They are already happening in places today and the benefits are being proven time and again. As trust in these types of systems increase, so too will the scope of their deployments. As the cost of physical goods around the world continues to drop, the relative sacrifice required for their redistribution will decrease correspondingly. In combination with the benefits of automated deployment, it is not difficult to imagine how systems will emerge that maximize society-wide benefit, rather than solely serving the desires of the richest or most well-connected.

Chapter 11

The Potential Impact of AI on Society

The previous two chapters explored a number of fields that will be radically transformed over the coming years and decades by the rising tide of AI. While the impact on broader society from the upheaval in any one of those industries is not fully clear, some broad trends do begin to emerge: AI will have a profound impact on core elements of our world, including jobs, consumption, civics, and even what it means to be a person.

In this chapter, I will explore some of these potential societal impacts, separate from any particular technology- or industry-focused change. The timelines for these impacts are intentionally left vague; there is too much uncertainty in the pace of both the development of underlying AI technology and its adoption by society. Still, it is time to spend more time talking about all of these issues (and how to prepare for them) now.

Jobs

It's hard to talk about the high-level impact of AI on society without starting with jobs. It's top-of-mind for most people within the tech world and many from without. And not without reason: previous technology revolutions have had substantial impacts on labor markets. The industrial revolution gutted the farm labor market. The past few decades have seen a drastic decrease in relative employment in factories. There is sufficient evidence from the past to suggest AI could have a meaningful impact on employment.

Types of jobs

The disruptive potential of AI is so great that very few argue that labor markets will look the same even a decade from now. While plenty may express optimism in the overall labor market, virtually everyone who has given the topic thought acknowledges that AI and automation will shift the distribution of jobs sooner rather than later.

Much AI today is being developed with "augmentation" in mind: the technology will sit alongside human workers who will leverage it to become better at what they do. In this world, job titles may not shift so much as job responsibilities: human workers will rely on AI for routine or data-intensive tasks, freeing themselves up for more abstract problem solving or human interaction. This type of AI will likely impact most any job that makes use of some kind of computer (large screen or otherwise).

Automation-focused AI will have a different impact: it will eliminate jobs. Most of this type of intelligence has been in factories to-date. While this type of technology often leads to the need for new jobs (machine maintenance, algorithm development, etc.), those jobs are not always viable for the employees who have been displaced.

In the short-run, augmentation is likely to be the dominant driver of workplace changes. However, automation is already very real in several industries and is likely to become more prevalent.

Overall, jobs will become more scarce when the required tasks are repetitive. Today's AI struggles with novelty, but excels at doing the same (or similar) thing over and over. This type of intelligent work is becoming more and more powerful in both the physical and cognitive realms.

As rote work is taken over, it is very likely that new opportunities will arise for non-routine work. Intelligent algorithms need designers, engineers, implementers, and maintainers. Even in non-digital roles, AI may allow professionals to shift from mixed routine/non-routine work to more purely non-rote as automation or augmentation take over the mundane tasks.

The types of non-routine work that are more resistant to automation require more education and training than the work that is being replaced. To prepare for this labor shift, our society must invest in giving that training to those most likely to need it: the people being displaced by AI (drivers, retail workers, customer service agents, fast food workers). Millions of workers will find the work they do today disappearing. Without proper education and training, we will face a serious employment crisis.

Total job availability

It is virtually inevitable that augmentation AI will give way to automation over time. It's a question of sophistication: while technology may not be advanced enough today to take over an entire job, there is no clear ceiling to the progress of the technology. An algorithm that can do 30% of a job today will be able to do 80% 10 years from now.

Even if new opportunities are created to match the pace of job loss, there is likely to be some inefficiency in between. Although the U.S. job market eventually recovered from the migration of agricultural jobs to industrial, there was substantial pain and unemployment as the transition occurred. In that case, the change was relatively gradual: the economy had several decades to adjust. There is a very real risk that an even greater transition could occur over even less time with the AI revolution.

To make matters worse, there is no guarantee that this labor disruption will be like past ones. In fact, I'm inclined to think that it won't be. When the automobile displaced the horse, there was a clear opportunity for drivers to transition their careers. That opportunity is much less obvious for drivers when delivery and transportation is automated *entirely*. The same is true for the various service industry jobs that are being automated as you read this.

Even if the 1+-for-1 job creation standard from the past holds in the short to medium term, it is not clear that it can continue to do so indefinitely. The purpose of AI is to perform human-level work. If it can do so at a fraction of the cost of a human, then is it really reasonable to believe that there will *always* be more work for displaced humans to do?

I think there is a very real possibility that *necessary* work available for humans to do will begin to decrease within the coming generation or two as AI gets closer and closer to general human intelligence. The question of what we should do when there really *aren't* jobs for people to perform is one that we should be giving more thought to.

Work in a post-scarcity society

In some ways, the relentless progress of technology can be framed as an effort to reduce (and eventually eliminate) scarcity. Scarcity is the phenomenon that we want more than we have. More food, more shelter, more money, more medicine, more toys. Just more.

AI is a continuation of that effort: whether automating or augmenting, AI is helping us produce more with the same amount (or less) of human effort. There is no clear upper bound on the potential for AI to ameliorate the problem of scarcity. While some people believe that AI will never achieve human-level intelligence, there is no widely-regarded compelling reason to believe that is the case (most rationale in that direction is more spiritual than logical).

There is a very real possibility that AI may make work as we know it today obsolete. If technology is performing all the work we need to have an abundance of real-world goods like food and medicine, then humans would not *need* to work at all. More specifically, there is a real possibility that AI could move us to that post-scarcity society *within the next 50 years*.

This possibility gives rise to a very fundamental "What's next?" question for us as a race. There is good reason[9] to believe that "work" is necessary for society: it gives us purpose and meaning. Without that purpose, we may find that things begin to crumble.

There are many proposed solutions to the sub-problems of the lack of work needed in a post-scarcity society: universal basic income, human augmentation (mostly via chip implants), redefining where we derive meaning, and changing "work" into tasks where machines are excluded (eSports, athletic sports, human services, etc.). All have their pros and cons. All are mostly untested today.

Prices of goods

With the concern on the jobs front, it can be easy to forget that there are a lot of good reasons that AI is advancing. Not least of these is that all of this automation and augmentation means that we can make more with less. As AI progresses, we will likely see the prices of most physical goods (and services!) coming down substantially in relative terms.

Reduction in prices of goods over time

The whole point of using technology to help us make and do things is to make those things cheaper and better. A standard shirt in the medieval times would cost about $500 assuming today's average wages[10]. Even more recently, the cost of a TV has dropped by over 90% in real terms over the past 20 years. We're getting much better at making and doing things all the time.

Advancing AI will continue this trend. It will automate the manual labor required to make things and the cognitive tasks required to manage that labor. It will allocate resources more effectively and design processes more efficiently. As they have over the previous couple of decades, the real prices of food, building materials, furniture, electronics, industrial equipment, and almost everything will continue to drop in the coming years.

There are a few notable exceptions to these decreasing prices: healthcare, education, and land. Millions of people are hard at work bringing the efficiencies seen elsewhere to healthcare and education. The rising cost of land is mostly driven by demand for *particular* land (namely in cities), rather than any real shortage of it around the world. This trend could be partially reversed with the advent of autonomous vehicles (which decrease the costs of commuting).

While there are potential shortages of physical resources at the micro-industry scale, as a whole the decreasing prices are likely to keep going down. We will likely transition almost completely to renewable energy before we run out of fossil fuels.

Non-renewable minerals are still available in abundance and—as crazy as it sounds—we will probably be able to mine them from other bodies in space before we run short on Earth.

The implication of all of this is that we will have more of just about everything in western society. Bigger houses, better cars, more entertainment. In the developing world, the impact will be two-fold: 1) they will benefit from the same advancing technologies in production that the developed world has without the investment in intermediate steps (this is known as "leapfrog" technology) and 2) the abundance in the developed world will be cheaper to allocate to the developing world.

Goods in a post-scarcity society

As mentioned in the previous section, there is a real possibility that all of this development results in a post scarcity society, where all basic human needs are met at virtually no cost. That is a hard world to imagine for us today. Soup kitchens may merge with a basic form of restaurant. Basic housing may be available for anyone who wants to move in. On-demand vehicles may be available to anyone for a guaranteed amount of time each month.

Even in that post-scarcity world, it is likely that society will not become completely egalitarian. I imagine that we will always find ways to stratify ourselves into "haves" and "have nots". The difference is that the distinction may not exist except at the highest level of Maslow's Hierarchy. The "haves" can show off their rare cars and works of art while food, shelter, and medical care are available in abundance to everyone.

It's worth noting that current distribution models are likely insufficient to achieve this type of widely distributed "wealth" without some kind of intermediary mechanism (like universal basic income).

Politics/economics

As AI continues to reshape our world, we will need to begin to rethink many of the basic tenants of our society. While the benefits of an AI-first world are multitudinous, it's unlikely that those benefits will be equitably distributed with our current systems. In the face of AI-fueled abundance, it will no longer be collectively conscionable to tolerate poverty due to an individual's circumstances. The general trend toward socialization that has gained momentum in the developed world over the past couple of decades will continue, driven by a relative abundance of goods and resources.

AI as a system of allocation

Today, in the United States and much of the rest of the developed world, capitalism is the primary system for determining the allocation of resources to individuals. Work more, earn more money, buy more things. The system has glaring failures from time to time that are corrected through government regulation, but overall the economy is left to its own devices. Fair or not, this system has proved the most effective to-date at achieving overall prosperity at scale.

Capitalism has thrived because it requires no overriding authority: resources are allocated by micro actions at a local scale. In general, transactions only occur when they are mutually beneficial to the participating parties. Major inefficiencies (outright theft or exploitation) are generally highly visible and can be policed. Minor inefficiencies often go uncorrected, but are not so costly as to ruin the overall system.

While this system generally works, the details leave much to be desired. Power dynamics and information asymmetry mean that exploitation is still commonplace. The increasing barriers to highly-efficient work mean that the rich are empowered to continue getting richer while the poor are often shut out from the fruits of technological progress.

Above all else, the current economic system is flawed because it is not a perfect agent of its true purpose. Overall, the purpose of our economic and political systems is to improve collective happiness, satisfaction, and utility. While these outcomes are mostly correlated with economic gain, the connection is not perfect. And while rewarding individuals for their work is a good principle, it fails at the margins: people who are less capable of working or whose talents are less likely to be directly rewarded in the way that something like an hour of programming is.

Artificial intelligence offers the opportunity to transcend the restrictions that make capitalism today's ideal solution. While we don't have the capacity for centralized management of resources today, this is exactly the type of problem that optimization and intelligent algorithms are designed to address at scale.

While general AI-fueled abundance *could* be distributed with today's patchwork system of welfare programs and charity, there is an opportunity to do much better. As a society, we will have an opportunity to shift our reward function from recognizing skills that can make money to those that maximize other overall societal outcomes (happiness, health, satisfaction, etc.).

To be sure, today it is uncertain what exactly a universal allocation AI might optimize for. That will require a great deal of debate and testing. Still, it is clear that today's systems fall short in very obvious ways at the macro scale: about a third of all U.S. corporate profit comes from the finance sector and the vast majority of income growth over the past decade has accumulated to the top 1%. These types of overall system imbalances suggest the potential for direction from a central intelligent authority with well-thought-out objectives.

AI as a decision-maker

If capitalism is a poor proxy for optimal resource allocation, then the current U.S. political system is a blatant affront to representing the welfare of the country's population. Representative democracy has proven a more fair and resilient system than any other form of government to-date, but is still rife with corruption, biased interests, and short-sightedness. The U.S. in particular is subject to the influence of money on decision-making, a phenomenon that exacerbates the system imbalances mentioned previously.

Sufficiently intelligent software has the potential to alleviate many of the weaknesses of our current system. AI can more accurately represent the interests of its constituents through a balanced evaluation model combined with a fair mechanism for gathering input. It can be distanced from the influencing effects of money by being carefully programmed to not care about money (or money's follow-on effects).

While the potential is massive, the prospect of handing decision-making authority over to a non-human must be approached with great care. There are already examples of such systems failing on small scales today. Intelligent systems that provide recommendations for sentencing of convicted criminals show clear signs of bias and perpetuating existing power structures. Algorithms that evaluate an applicant's credit-worthiness have no human compassion for unavoidable circumstances or personal growth and development.

As AI takes a more prominent role in making decisions, it is inevitable that it will cause problems, even as overall outcomes improve. It is important that diverse peoples and perspectives are brought together in the design of these systems and that their performance is openly and regularly evaluated to maximize equity. It will also be critically important for the foreseeable future to incorporate appeal processes with manual human review as part of any automated decision-making.

War

Outside of perhaps job loss, the prospect of AI being used in war is the public's greatest concern about the rise of artificial intelligence. Fears are fed by popular science fiction like *Terminator* and *The Matrix*. The plot is well-known by now: humans make AI, AI decides humans shouldn't exist, then AI declares war, often begun with some kind of mass-killing event.

As practical AI has risen in the public consciousness over the past few years, headlines about AI turning on us have been relatively uncommon, at least in comparison with the thousands of stories on more practical AI tackling everyday problems. As such, the AI backlash that many predicted around 2015 has not occurred: the public hasn't risen up against researchers and demanded that they cease all work on intelligent algorithms.

In fact, public reaction to some truly concerning events has been more muted than almost anyone expected. Tesla's autopilot functionality has now been responsible for several driver and passenger deaths. An autonomous Uber vehicle hit and killed a pedestrian. Microsoft's public Tay chatbot became virulently racist almost overnight. While all of these events have been taken seriously by practitioners in the industry, they've barely warranted a second thought from most people outside of the tech (and automotive) industry.

The reality is that the dangers of AI are very real and—in the long-term—hard to predict. While that danger is present everywhere that AI is having an impact, it has received surprisingly little attention in the most obvious high-risk area: warfare.

AI is a reality in warfare today. Facial recognition, drones, cruise missiles, autonomous land vehicles. Let's not forget that DARPA's (a U.S. defense agency) Grand Challenges in 2004-2007 are what gave rise to the reality of driverless cars today.

Given the application of AI in today's combat environment—and especially because of the relative lack of attention it's garnered—we as a society should be paying more attention to what an AI-first future looks like for warfare.

War by proxy

One of the most obvious ways that AI is transforming the battlefield is by enabling sophisticated powers to wage war by proxy: utilizing intelligent machines to do fighting that would otherwise require humans. Bomb robots, drones, and intelligent missiles are all examples of how armed forces are now beginning to rely on software to make decisions so that humans don't have to be in harm's way.

In many ways, the replacement of humans with machines is a good thing. War is awful and human life is precious. If machine-first warfare decreases the loss of human life, then there is plenty of benefit. However, that benefit doesn't come without potential costs.

Armed forces are already relying on software to make decisions about killing today. That reliance is in its earliest stages: a human is always *somewhere* in the chain of decision-making and AI is still only playing a supporting role. However, it's nearly inevitable that AI will be making more and more decisions about when to pull the trigger. Handing matters of life and death over to non-humans is a matter that we should all take *very* seriously. Humans have the capability to exercise their own judgment: to disobey an order or call off a mission. Software—for the most part—doesn't. It does what it's programmed to do. Something akin to "judgment" can be programmed in, but we had better be *very* sure that artificial judgment is a suitable replacement for humanity before entrusting it with lives.

Another potential downside of the separation of humans from war is that it lowers the cost of waging war in the first place. Relative conflict around the world has dropped over time in no small part because the pain it causes has become more well-known: battlefields can now be televised and recorded. Nearly everyone in the world has been exposed to graphic imagery of what it costs when their government declares war.

The emotional and human cost of losing machines in a battle can't be compared with the loss of human life. To a much greater extent, war could become a matter of money and other resources. With the dehumanization of war comes the risk of an ensuing rise in conflict. If the machine-focused conflict stays away from humans, then that future may be preferable. But it seems highly likely that the violence would spill over and even more innocent lives would be put in danger than with today's environment.

Cyber warfare

The past decade or so has seen the rise of a new phenomenon: nation-level conflict playing out in the digital world. The U.S.- and Israeli-developed Stuxnet worm, which caused substantial damage to Iran's nuclear program, is one of the most famous examples. Russian interference in the 2016 U.S. presidential election is another massive instance.

Because it is so new, the implications of cyber warfare are not yet clear. The *possibilities*, however, are frightening. While it may be tempting to shrug off cyber warfare as "oh well, I'll get a new computer", the reality is significantly more dangerous. The reality of modern society is that the physical world relies on the digital. It is not particularly hard to imagine a cyber attack causing power outages or other infrastructure failures that result in real pain and death. That may even be less catastrophic than more subtle attacks focused on destabilizing world powers.

One of the truly concerning aspects of cyber warfare is that it has not yet developed the same sorts of international taboos that conventional warfare has. Despite clear evidence of nations launching cyberattacks on each other, the response from the international community has been muted. The clear message is that while physical military action will not be tolerated, the digital world is an open battleground ripe for a dominant technical power.

Already, AI is shaping the landscape of cyber warfare. Nation-scale misinformation campaigns are only possible through automation. The intelligence required to crack sophisticated digital defenses must often be autonomous, as a worm or virus must adapt to a situation without being able to communicate back to its originator. And this type of intelligence is being pursued fairly openly: the first DARPA Cyber Grand Challenge took place in the summer of 2016, when seven autonomous computer agents competed to hack each other for a prize.

The international community is ill-equipped to handle cyber warfare today. It barely understands the field and does not have the tools to either identify it or properly assign accountability when it happens. In this environment, global powers like the U.S., Russia, and China are allowed to pursue weapons development with almost no inhibition. The prospects for the future of cyber warfare are grim unless we can figure out how to reign in its wanton progress.

Potential for an extinction event

While it has become gauche for anyone within the tech community to talk seriously about the risk of AI "turning on us", the long-term possibility is worth considering. As discussed elsewhere in this book, there is no convincing reason to believe that AI will not surpass human-level intelligence within the next 100 years. When it does so, we will not be able to think of it as "just a computer" any longer: AI will then have the ability to act independently and pursue its own objectives.

If AI with greater-than-human intelligence also has control of weapons (conventional or digital), we should be rightly afraid of what it might do with them. While an irradiated planet would be uninhabitable for humans, machines do not have the same restrictions. It is not safe to assume that software will have the same compunctions against using weapons of mass destruction that humans have; respect for human life is a uniquely human characteristic, AI won't *necessarily* have it.

There are no simple solutions to the prospect of AI's potential to cause the extinction of humanity. It is clear that we are past the point of no return: AI will continue to develop around the world regardless of any restrictions levied by individual governing bodies. Nor is AI development necessarily susceptible to the same kinds of controls that nuclear, chemical, and biological materials are: software is generally much easier to program for individuals and small groups than those rare and costly resources.

Because there is no obvious solution, it is very important that we have more serious high-level dialogue about the risks—and correct approaches—of developing ever-more-intelligent software. The majority of practitioners today are failing on even basic ethical considerations of AI development; why should we think that they'll do better when the considerations involve human life at a massive scale?

Machine rights

Humans occupy a unique position on Earth as the only rational beings. While we recognize the emotions, intelligence, and perhaps even consciousness of other animals, we hold humans above all others because of their unique capabilities of cognition. We afford humans unique rights because of that difference. No other animal is granted the near-universal right to life or independence, though many more intelligent animals like apes, dolphins, and octopi do have some protections.

To the extent that intelligence is the driving force for the granting of rights, the advancement of artificial intelligence will give rise to very deep questions about what types of entities deserve what rights.

Non-organic sentience

"Sentience" is the capability to feel or experience the world subjectively. There is no such thing as inorganic sentience today: machines do exactly what they are programmed to do (even if it doesn't always feel that way to the programmer). Their experience is not subjective; they behave according to predefined rules.

As AI advances, it will begin to test the boundaries of this historical paradigm. It's not clear at what point something goes from "not sentient" to "sentient", but most people would agree that a single-celled prokaryote isn't while a dog is. The general state of AI's advancement is also somewhere in that murky middle ground today. No AI is capable of the complex and dynamic expression of a dog *today*, but it seems unlikely that such a development is much more than a decade or two away.

When AI achieves the general level of intelligence and adaptability of animals like dogs, we must begin to question what rights they might be entitled to. Advanced animals are often protected by laws to prevent cruelty. Might there be some kind of AI anti-cruelty counterpart? If so, it's not entirely clear what "cruelty" might be for AI. A sufficiently extreme stimulus that hinders its ability to optimize its objective function? AI won't necessarily have any kind of equivalent to "pain" as organic entities feel it; pain is only a near-universal companion to sentience because they both rely on an advanced organic nervous system.

As discussed elsewhere in this book, there is no compelling reason to believe that AI won't eventually achieve human-level intelligence. In preparation for that possibility, the conversation must evolve from "any rights" to "which rights". It is possible that it is our species' intelligence which entitles us to the rights we hold, in which case a machine with greater-than-human intelligence may be entitled to just as many rights as any human. It is also possible that society decides there is some other aspect of humanity that justifies human-level rights, in which case artificially sentient entities will be excluded.

While the discussion of theoretical rights for hypothetical future artificial intelligence is important, it is worth remembering that the subject of *human* rights is far from settled.

The fight for systemic and practical equality for people from all kinds of groups very much rages on. Atrocities are committed against people—and rights are denied—all across the world every day. The conversation about rights for non-human entities should not detract from the very real human suffering that still exists.

Possible rights

Few rights are held more sacred than the right to life. While that right could be construed to apply only in a biological sense, most people interpret this right to imply the continued existence of their consciousness: the difference between death and a vegetative state is minimal to most. In the case of AI, the right to life might be better termed as a right to exist.

Even just the right to exist is highly problematic for software. It certainly does not have that right today (programmers stop and delete software constantly). If AI were to be granted such a right, at what point would the right kick in? Does the right to exist also imply a right to the resources *necessary* for existence, such as electricity and hardware to run on? This might be compared to a right to food and shelter for humans, but that right is far from universal in modern society. On the other hand, what good is a right to exist if a server operator can end an AI's existence with the flip of a switch if it doesn't pay its power bill?

The second most universal right is that of independence. It is a right that has historically been denied to millions—and millions more have died to claim or protect. Does a sufficiently advanced AI have a right to independence or does it always belong to whomever created it?

Behind the right to independence are a series of ever-more-complicated follow on questions and rights. If an artificially sentient entity has the right to independence, does it have the right to privacy? While this right is far from guaranteed to many humans, most modern society has at least *some* protection around its citizens' privacy. Similarly, does an independent AI have the right to own property? Again, this is a right that was denied to *most* humans at many times throughout history. And yet, we now recognize that every person has the right to build their own wealth (and that this is, in fact, fundamental to independence).

There is no end to the questions around appropriate rights for a sufficiently advanced AI. Can they be citizens of a country? Can they hold jobs? Can they sue others in the court system? The only thing that is certain is that our society today is completely unequipped to answer any of these questions. That's not awful; the questions aren't relevant today as the first sentient AIs are still years away. Still, the atrocities that have been committed against humans (and other animals) should serve as a warning that it's better to think about these issues proactively rather than reactively.

Practical vs. moral reasoning

When it comes to rights for humans and other animals, the conversation mostly centers on moral reasoning: it's *wrong* to enslave a person or to torture an animal. That's a good thing. Morals exist to protect us and make sure that everyone has a chance, even when Darwinism might argue against those who don't have the power to defend themselves.

As the conversation on rights for AI evolves, it will undoubtedly take on moral tones. Perhaps it will be considered *wrong* to turn off a sufficiently advanced AI. Again, that may be a good thing: if we determine that intelligence is what calls for rights, then a sufficiently advanced AI deserves to be protected. However, the moral argument is not the only one.

Even without moral reasoning, it may prove prudent to grant rights to sufficiently advanced AI. Practically speaking, it may be better for us humans. The right to exist provides the best illustration.

The AI doomsday scenario feels familiar to pretty much everyone: humans build AI, which then decides the best way to do what it was programmed to do is to kill all the humans. In many cases, the mechanism for this polar shift is when the AI realizes that its human handlers can turn it off at any point. Obviously it can't do what it was programmed to do if it doesn't exist, so it develops a type of self preservation that fuels its murderous rampage.

In the science fiction stories that hinge on an AI doomsday, guarantees of the AI's right to exist are virtually nonexistent. Of course, we shouldn't rely too heavily on the example provided by fiction, but it is possible that guaranteeing advanced AI the right to exist could provide a protection mechanism against it developing the desire to get rid of all of us.

Malevolent superintelligence

Up until now, this book has (hopefully) managed to keep its warning tone about the dangers of AI somewhere short of shrill. This section gives into the fear-mongering for just a minute and explores the possibility of AI becoming evil and deciding it wants to take over the world.

The potential for super-powerful AI with ill intent has been explored in depth by science fiction and by futurists. It's the reason that Elon Musk spearheaded the $1B commitment to found OpenAI (and maybe why he wants to set up a colony on Mars?). Nick Bostrom dedicated 353 long pages to detailing just how we could prevent such an AI from killing us in *Superintelligence*. All of these warnings have struck a nerve with the public consciousness: even if more-than-half-kidding, just about anyone can have a decent conversation about the possibility of AI wiping out the human race.

But for the most part, all of the warnings have not generated particularly *serious* conversation. There is no real cry to prevent the use of AI in warfare. No discussions of limits on the advancement of faster hardware or more complex algorithms. No practical plans to implement anything that Bostrom laid out.

My hope with this section of the book is to shift the dialogue around AI as a real threat to humanity toward a more serious tone. While even the most aggressive projections of artificial superintelligence place it decades in the future, the reality is that we need as much of that time as possible to prepare.

Possibility

A fair number of technologists and researchers do not believe that there is meaningful risk of AI ever developing the capability or will to kill all humans. However, their evidence for this belief does not measure up against the cost of being wrong. Admittedly, there is no concrete evidence that AI can become smarter than humans. Likewise, there is no evidence that it *can't*. The reality is that we still have a very poor theoretical understanding of what human-level intelligence even *is*, much less how we might replicate it.

As fuel in their argument, AGI doubters point at the various misfires and inconsistent progress in AI's development since the middle of the century. Indeed, regardless of when asked, there always seems to be a general sentiment that human-level AI is about 20 years[11] in the future.

These arguments miss two key points. The first is that despite wide fluctuations in public interest, the progress in AI over the decades has been remarkably steady. While people's *caring* has varied substantially, the underlying technology has consistently advanced. The second—and more important— oversight is that the evidence for AGI being 20 years away has never been stronger. Where predictions from the 60s and 80s relied on gut feel, the reality is that we're now about 20 years away from having the hardware that could model deep neural networks on the scale of the human brain (roughly 500 trillion synapses).

Of course, deep neural networks are not a perfect replica of the human brain. Critics rightly point out that creating a DNN the size of a human brain won't necessarily result in incredible intelligence. This criticism goes too far, however, in writing off the risk. While the link between intelligence and DNN size may not be 1-for-1, there is plenty of evidence that larger DNNs are capable of greater feats of artificial intelligence[12]. There is also evidence that *humans* don't actually need as much brain capacity as is generally expected[13].

Much of the dismissal of the risk of super bad AI focuses on its timeline: why worry about AI's risk decades from now when it's causing real societal harm today? The underlying concern is absolutely appropriate: we should be paying more attention to how we use sophisticated algorithms at scale to minimize negative impact today. But the two are not mutually exclusive. AI is important enough to us as a society that we should make cognitive room for both considerations.

Part of the problem with ignoring the risk of ASI "just for now" is that we don't know *when* the right time to worry will be. As previously mentioned, it is hard to predict exactly when AI will begin to reach human levels. Preparing now means we'll be ready whenever it does happen. Not preparing now runs the risk of not being prepared at all, and having to play catch up as AI outstrips our ability to work with it.

Potential for an extinction event

If you accept that AI will eventually surpass human-level intelligence, then the question remains: can (or will) it destroy humanity?

The answer to the "can" of the question seems to fairly apparently be "yes" unless proactive defensive measures are implemented. Even if it could only achieve human-level intelligence, the replicability and speed of decision-making possible to computers mean that we should be pretty concerned about AGI's capability to cause us harm. Without very well-designed systems, it seems highly likely that sufficiently intelligent software could hide its activity from observers until its ability to manipulate the world (both physical and digital) was virtually unassailable.

In terms of the will to cause humans harm, the answer is a bit murkier. It just depends on how the AI is programmed and how its intelligence emerges. It's certainly plausible that all sufficiently advanced AI will be developed to be altruistic: exclusively helping humans rather than harming them. That outcome, however, requires a level of optimism that previous technological progress doesn't necessarily warrant. Chemical weapons were used by all sides before being banned. The US dropped two atomic bombs on civilian populations before the world realized what an atrocity nuclear weapons were. It doesn't seem like much of a stretch to believe that dangerous AI might be developed before the implications of its existence were fully understood.

To me, it seems obvious that there is some non-zero chance that AI develops with the will and means to end humanity in the next century. I'm not sure how high that probability is. Whatever it is, any likelihood of an extinction event on that time horizon would seem to warrant more attention than I think we have seriously given it up until now.

Chapter 12

How to Pursue AI Ethically

Throughout this book I've talked about the incredible changes that AI will have on our world and how to pursue its development. This chapter builds on that foundation: it is not sufficient simply to know how to apply AI; you must also know how to apply it *in the right way*. The disruptive power of AI is too great to be employed with anything less than a thorough consideration of ethics and morality.

This is the single most important chapter of the book. Previous chapters have hopefully made it clear that AI has near-unlimited potential to reshape our world. The past has shown us that we cannot simply trust that those seeking technological advancement will employ it responsibly; much of the last century has been lived in fear of nuclear holocaust. How much of that fear and danger could have been avoided if the power of nuclear energy had been developed in a more responsible manner?

Given its importance, there's a real argument that I should have begun this book with a discussion on the ethics of building AI systems. But I think the discussion would have been premature at that point: even knowing the potential dangers of AI requires a foundational understanding of the technology itself. Without that understanding, any rules of thumb regarding building AI come off as little more than platitudes: only build AI to help humanity, be completely transparent about your models' parameters, that sort of thing. Such an unnuanced approach has dominated the industry recently: business leaders have thrown out pithy "rules of AI" that don't hold up to the realities of building software in the real world.

The hope is that with your new-found understanding of how to build AI systems and where they can be applied, you are prepared to think about the downsides of using this knowledge in the wrong way. You're ready to begin a journey of learning how to be an ethical AI practitioner.

Just because you can doesn't mean you should

One of the many great quotes from *Jurassic Park* comes when Goldblum's character first sees evidence of the park's dinosaurs: "Your scientists were so preoccupied with whether or not they could, they didn't stop to think if they should." The line is melodramatic and completely wrong: dinosaurs are awesome, of course we should figure out how to bring them back.

The same kind of unmitigated excitement doesn't hold for AI. There are a lot of things that the new technology *can* do, but what *should* it do? This line of thinking is shockingly lacking for many of the projects being pursued today. High profile projects have sought to determine a person's sexuality[14] or their "objective" attractiveness[15]. Police forces have begun experimenting with facial recognition as a criminal investigation tool, with some disastrous consequences[16].

Technology is not morally neutral. Developing solutions that decrease hunger are better than solutions that promote violence or reduce civil liberties. As a practitioner making use of AI to affect the world, it is in your hands to ensure that the solutions you develop are used in good ways. As AI becomes more and more widespread, it will undoubtedly be deployed in ways that make the world worse. That makes it all the more important that the vast majority of us are thoughtful about what we're doing and why. The risks of misapplying AI at scale are too great for us to carelessly advance the technology without heed for how it will be used.

To be clear, I believe it is the moral responsibility of AI practitioners to decline to work on exciting technical problems where there is disproportionate risk for misapplication. Facial recognition provides a prime example. Both Google and

Facebook have developed facial recognition algorithms with superhuman performance under specific circumstances. Following their success, such algorithms are now rampant across the technical world: they're being deployed by governments ranging from the UK to China, with clear abuses of civil rights already occurring. While the original Facebook researchers may have just been concerned with making tagging pictures easier, the potential for abuse of their findings would have been obvious from the get-go.

Figuring out the risks of any given AI technology is not easy. While facial recognition may seem obvious, how about an entertaining chatbot? It almost certainly didn't occur to anyone at Microsoft that Tay might turn into a vehicle for delivering hatred and bigotry. But just because they didn't foresee the problem doesn't mean they *couldn't* have. Online abuse and trolling is not a rare problem; it probably just hadn't happened in any particularly virulent form to the members of Tay's development team.

The coming sections will lay out some of the methods you can apply to make sure that you're picking the right problems to pursue and doing so in a responsible way.

Make sure you're optimizing for the right problem

Let's say you have the blueprint to implement an AI system that can determine the guilt of a suspect in a crime when they give their testimony under oath. Perhaps the technology analyzes their voice or their facial expressions while sleeping (this technology already exists). Let's say you test the model on a thousand samples, distributed evenly (500/500) between suspects who were found guilty and those were exonerated. The model successfully identifies 490 of the truly guilty suspects as guilty and only incorrectly flags 15 of those who were let off.

Is this a good model? Should you publicize it? Should you make it available for use in real trials, as one of the tools available to both prosecution and defense?

The intuitive answer is "yes" (at least it is for me). Such a model is very accurate (as far as similarly complex models are concerned) and can go a long way in removing more real criminals from society.

To bring clarity to the question, I would ask another one: what is the objective function? What are you trying to minimize or maximize with this AI system? It seems obvious that the answer is you're trying to maximize the chance of correctly identifying a criminal. But is that really the objective?

The United States has a clearly defined burden of evidence in criminal cases: beyond a reasonable doubt. While the term is well defined, its mathematical definition is less so. 50% is certainly a reasonable doubt... what about 10%? 1%? 0.1%? According to most statisticians they're all "reasonable" doubts (to the extent that the term has any statistical meaning): they are non-zero and can be quantified.

While juries and judges aren't typically inclined to think in such quantitative terms, there is plenty of evidence to suggest the threshold for "beyond a reasonable doubt" is pretty high. Polygraphs are not permitted as evidence, despite the studies indicating they're fairly accurate (typically cited as ~70-90%). And while the 99.75% accuracy of the "guiltiness" detector from before is well above that threshold, is that actually the *relevant* accuracy? The test set was equally split between positives and negatives (as many machine learning test sets are). But that test set is not even slightly indicative of the broader population. The 3% false positive rate would result in over 10 *million* wrongful convictions if it were applied blindly across the United States population.

The question of whether or not you should publicize the guiltiness detector is not a purely quantitative one. There's no clear threshold at which the detector is "good" instead of "bad". Instead, its impact on society must be assessed in context. We know that the purpose of the U.S. criminal justice system isn't to maximize the imprisonment of criminals, but what is it? As far as I know, there is no clearly quantified answer.

One approach for evaluating the morality of the guilt detector is evaluating its performance versus its alternative. In this case, would the guilt detector increase or decrease the wrongful conviction rate of innocent defendants? If the research showed that 5% of criminal convictions were actually in error and that the 3% false positive rate from the model drew exclusively from this population, then there would be considerably more evidence that the AI system was providing a net good.

Figuring out the right problem to solve (or the right objective function) is not always easy. Criminal justice is just one of many examples that are fraught with emotion and passion and the most obvious answer isn't necessarily the right one. There's no secret to figuring out what the right answer is. Generally it takes much more work and a much broader perspective gathering than practitioners are wont to undertake if they are not placing the ethics of AI at the forefront.

Look out for biased data and models

Among casual observers or practitioners of statistics, there is a general sentiment that "numbers don't lie". The idea is that as long as your data is factually accurate, the insights it generates will be as well. Tempting as it may be, this way of thinking is utter nonsense.

While declining across the board, the arrest rate for marijuana for people with black skin in America is much higher than it is for people with white skin. Based on this data, the naive statistician might believe that black people smoke weed at a much higher rate than white people. They don't[17]. They're just policed more heavily and arrested for it more often.

Here's the danger: there are thousands of statisticians and AI practitioners operating today as if black people smoked more weed. They are systematizing and granting validity to systemic racism and injustice, all while feeling like they're making the world a better place. This perpetuation of bias can be seen clearly in crime prediction models and sentencing models, both of which are now used heavily in the criminal justice system and disproportionately affect people of color[18].

Because humans have limited cognitive computational power and access to information, we rely on heuristics for making decisions. These heuristics are vital to our functioning at every level. They also create bias. And bias creates injustice. These phenomena are rampant in the world around us. Part of the promise of AI is that it can bring more objectivity and impartiality to a world where bias has flourished, potentially bringing better, more equitable outcomes to all kinds of people. But it also has a very real, very dangerous potential to make bias worse than it is today.

Bias has been measured in automated decision-making processes of all kinds: lending[19], school admissions[20], criminal justice[18]. Everywhere that humans and historical data are involved, there's a real risk of perpetuating bias. In fact, I would argue that bias is the *default* state of many statistical models, rather than a rare and unfortunate side effect.

As a practitioner and implementer of AI solutions, it is vitally important to the health of our society that you cultivate a constant diligence against the dangers of bias. Avoid blindly baking in data that is commonly associated with discrimination (income, gender, race, zip code, etc.). Gather as many diverse perspectives as you can. Commit to periodically evaluating the impact of your model on all kinds of populations.

Commit to transparency

You may notice a theme emerging in my advice on how to pursue the development of AI ethically: gather a lot of different perspectives. That's because almost everyone building AI solutions is inherently good: they want to make the world a better place according to their values. "Bad" solutions typically come into existence because of a lack of perspective: the solution that works well for 70% of the population may be pretty bad for the remaining 30%.

Unfortunately, the currently dominant approach to AI development does not lend itself to perspective gathering. Many practitioners pursue their development in secret, worried that if their work gets out then others will steal it (or point out its flaws). This is a tricky problem because it's rooted in truth: once the world finds out a particular problem is solvable, it becomes much more likely to be solved by different parties even without any particular information about the solution.

The difficulty of this challenge doesn't mean we should just give up on transparency. In fact, it means that we should work even harder for it. But not in the superficial way that has become common over the past couple of years, where the worst offenders of developing black box solutions have called for blind, blanket commitments for AI researchers to be transparent.

The right solution around transparency must acknowledge that there *is* a time and place for secrecy. The ability to protect intellectual property is fundamental to advancement; it's impractical to believe that everyone will just open up the nitty gritty technical details of their most sophisticated models and datasets. But that need for protection must be balanced against the very real danger to society of the proliferation of inscrutable AI decision-makers.

At my company, 4Degrees, we're pretty open about the technology we're developing. We're generally happy to chat with investors, customers, and other practitioners about the models we use, where our data comes from, and our process for building solutions. We believe that the sharing of knowledge is a good unto itself and that our solutions will be improved by soliciting input from a variety of different perspectives. At the same time, we don't post our full datasets, models, and hyperparameters online for everyone to see. While these could all be reconstructed by a sufficiently motivated group, we don't think that there is much marginal value of transparency in this case, at least in comparison to the risk of making it *too* easy for would-be competitors to replicate our technology.

Opening up about advanced technology is made somewhat easier if its developers seek to create their defensible "moat" through overall experience instead of pure technical superiority. That is the approach we've taken at 4Degrees. On its own, not one of our AI models is a technical marvel (sadly, we haven't set any records for size or sophistication of deep reinforcement learning model). But taken together in combination with endless work on user experience, we've created something truly remarkable (and much harder to replicate!). In fact, this approach to differentiation is what allows us to feel comfortable talking so openly with the public about how we build our technology.

Fight closed feedback loops

The best machine learning models are plugged into their own outputs: the more they operate in the wild, the more they learn about how their environment works. While this architecture can lead to far more accurate and sophisticated outcomes over time, it can also lead to its own form of bias.

If a model is being used to inform decision-making, then it is a tautology that the model's "positives" will lead to one decision and its "negatives" to another. A good example might be a model evaluating whether or not to issue a mortgage to an applicant. That mortgage risk evaluation model might be improved over time by feeding back in "positives" who later defaulted on their loans. The model can take this data, re-evaluate its parameters, and then decide to issue fewer loans to similar candidates who may also be more likely to default.

The issue with these types of models (which are fairly common) is that they only learn from true positives and false positives: times when the model said "yes". They almost never learn anything from the negatives (the loan applicants that were rejected). False negatives are very hard to determine because upon a negative evaluation, the evaluatee typically leaves the system. In our loan case, even if the applicant successfully gets and repays a loan from another lender, the original lender who first declined them is very unlikely to ever learn of this "false negative".

Therein lies the problem for models with closed feedback loops. While they can get "smarter" over time, they also tend to perpetuate the status quo. A crime prediction system may become a self-fulfilling prophecy if it directs more police attention to a historically high-crime block—driving up arrest rates—while ignoring a previously quiet block that has seen a rash of recent crime.

The push here is not to ignore data that is generated after the implementation of a given model. Rather, it is to be thoughtful about the selection bias that may be inherent in that data. Where possible, seek out data that you can bring into the system to break the self-fulfilling nature of the closed feedback loop.

The role of humans in automated decision-making

AI—and more vanilla statistics—is taking a progressively more active role in automated decision-making. You can now be granted a credit card or insurance policy within seconds, your application completely untouched by human eyes. This automation has many benefits: it has brought more objectivity to decisions that were previously highly susceptible to bias and it has driven down the costs of administering many societal necessities.

Of course, these models are rarely (if ever) perfect. They'll make mistakes. They're just not sophisticated enough and don't have enough information to make the right decision every single time. And sometimes these mistakes can appear completely absurd to humans: algorithms don't "think" like humans do, so it's not surprising that they fail in very inhuman ways.

Particularly egregious failures of otherwise beneficial models can have serious negative consequences. The first is for those who pay the cost directly: the qualified applicant denied a loan because they have a common name or the 4.0 student rejected from their dream school because the model didn't recognize their grading scale. But an even greater failure can happen when these (hopefully) limited cases gain publicity. Due to the apparent "stupidity" of the evaluation model, the public can lose faith in its predictive power—and the predictive power of AI generally. Even when these too-simplistic models achieve much more accurate outcomes than humans can on their own, they may be dismantled because of emotional public reaction.

In most cases, this danger can be solved with a rather simple process tweak. Rather than making the output of the machine final and irrevocable, build in a manual appeal process that makes use of human judgment. With such a fix, the loan applicant's identity could be verified and the student's GPA could be accounted properly. While getting humans involved may increase the cost of evaluation, the hybrid system is still likely to be much cheaper than a fully manual process and doesn't run the risk of highly embarrassing failures that humans wouldn't make.

These human-augmented automation processes should dominate for the foreseeable future. While there will certainly be a time when AI systems can be reliably more accurate than a system with *any* human involvement, the reality is that intelligent systems are just too simple today. They can't account for all of the possible variations and externalities that humans can.

Issues of representation in AI development

This chapter has repeatedly talked about the importance of bringing diverse perspectives together to limit the negative fallout of AI poorly applied. For most projects, this should involve a formal effort with thoughtful evaluation of the perspectives to be included.

However, I'm not naive: it's incredibly unlikely that all AI projects will undertake the effort and investment of this perspective gathering. In fact, I'd be positively surprised if a majority of major projects instituted such a policy in the next five years. As such, there is a broader issue in the AI community that is contributing to less-than-ideal outcomes. Namely, most AI practitioners today are white men from similar backgrounds in the US, Canada, or England.

As a whole, today's AI practitioners have not been targeted for persecution by their governments or excluded from economic opportunity by their societies. The risk of "just math" applied in the wrong way doesn't feel nearly as real to them as it might to someone brought up in a family captured in the vicious cycle of payday loans or prisons. They probably weren't unfairly accused of shoplifting as teenagers. They probably haven't considered changing their name on their application to get a more fair shake from a hiring manager with 3 seconds to spend per resume. And they probably haven't been targeted for organized harassment online simply because of who they are.

Of course, that's not to say that white men are immune from any of these societal problems. They absolutely do happen. Just not with the regularity that they occur to more marginalized populations: people of color, the LGBTQ community, Muslims and Jews, women in tech. Due to the terrible potential for AI-at-scale to perpetuate discrimination, it is critically important that populations that have faced historical discrimination be included in all aspects of AI's development. Even with the best of intentions, a relatively homogenous group of people building AI solutions is less likely to reach an equitable and fair outcome than a group of people who bring a wider diversity of perspectives.

We are far from the optimal level of representational diversity in the field of AI today[21]. But all hope is not lost; some basic efforts will go a long way toward making the problem better. We should spend more time in underserved communities showing children the promise of AI and a career in the technology industry. We should widen our aperture for the "signals" that we look for in hiring, not just indexing on the same dozen universities or handful of tech giants. We should seek to cultivate a sense of belonging for *everyone* looking to get involved in the AI community.

Don't overstate your model's intelligence

Given the hype around the field of AI and how fast the technology is advancing, there is a very real incentive to overstate the capabilities of what you're developing. By juicing your system's performance marginally, you can sway a customer or investor who would have otherwise been on the fence. And the risk is relatively low: they probably won't know the difference—and who knows, you might actually achieve that level of performance by the time it matters.

You must resist the temptation. The field of AI today is plagued with half-truths and overhype. The potential of AI to change the world is truly magnificent, but it's also not always easy to understand. Misconstrued headlines and outright exaggeration can be found everywhere that there is discussion of AI. The field certainly doesn't need practitioners who actually know what they're talking about willfully inflating their accomplishments.

The danger of misleading everyone on the capabilities of your solutions is that if a lot of people are behaving similarly, it is inevitable that everyone will find out. While it's certainly possible that slight exaggeration can be overlooked occasionally, when it happens on an industry-wide scale it's tough to miss. There's plenty of that happening today. Some consultants and AI solution providers seek to avoid specific commitments on model outcomes or overshoot what's prudent when they do provide real numbers. The reality of the situation becomes obvious months or a couple of years later and faith is lost in the *general* capability of AI.

That's the real risk of overpromising on the capabilities of AI solutions. AI isn't a panacea for the world's problems today. Models are still fairly unsophisticated and adapt poorly to new environments. Even good AI solutions aren't going to solve all of the problems that they might be expected to.

If short-term expectations for AI are inflated beyond reality, then we're setting the industry up for an inevitable crash (or "bubble bursting"). To a significant extent, AI's progress relies on the continued faith and investment of society. If everyone feels betrayed by inflated expectations that can't live up to reality, then they may lose their enthusiasm for AI investment.

Even ignoring previous AI winters, we're already beginning to see this play out. Anecdotally, much of IBM's early investment into—and sales of—its Watson platform didn't produce the Earth-shaking results that they had expected (or at least promised). In response, early adopters and observers of Watson's product lost some of their initial enthusiasm for investing in AI technologies at the cutting edge.

Many AI practitioners—particularly academics—feel that overhype is the greatest risk facing the field of AI today. They worry about the risk of a new AI winter brought on by the inability for technology to keep pace with sensationalist headlines in the short-run. I don't necessarily agree that overhype is the *biggest* threat facing the field... the risk to society of AI poorly-applied seems far more dangerous. But I am certainly excited by the investment pouring into the space right now and would be disappointed to see that take a hit because of ill-advised marketing.

Reference Lists

Case Studies

Logic Theorist

The Logic Theorist is widely considered to be the first recognized piece of AI software. It was developed by Allen Newell, Herbert Simon, and Cliff Shaw and presented at the 1956 Dartmouth AI conference.

The Logic Theorist made use of symbolic logic to prove mathematical theorems. It eventually 38 of the first 52 theorems in *Principia Mathematica*; some of its proofs were more elegant than those previously accepted.

The Logic Theorist is partially responsible for the wave of interest in AI around the 1960s, particularly to the extent that the interest centered around symbolic logic systems.

OCR at the post office

The United States Postal Service was one of the earliest and most successful adopters of AI technology. The post office began experimenting with mechanization for letter sorting in 1956. They implemented the first high speed OCR (optical character recognition) system in Detroit in 1965.

Full automation of mail sorting began in 1982 in LA, when a single-line OCR system was combined with an extended zip code to eliminate the need for any address reading by humans. Today, mail sorting is almost entirely automated across the developed world.

Deep Blue vs. Kasparov

There were two six game matches between Garry Kasparov (then world champion of chess) and IBM-developed

Deep Blue, a chess-playing artificial intelligence, in 1996 and 1997. Kasparov defeated Deep Blue in 1996, but lost in 1997.

Deep Blue's victory was originally heralded as a sign of great advancement in computers' ability to mimic human intelligence. In later years, however, the significance of the victory on the AI world was downplayed. Kasparov's play during the 1997 match was widely considered to be sub-par for the champion and the methods Deep Blue used to achieve its victory were criticized as mere brute force.

Deep Blue's primary advantage over previous chess-playing AIs was its capability to perform massive tree searches: evaluating millions of positions for the expected value of any given move.

Watson on *Jeopardy!*

Inspired by their previous success with Deep Blue and by the dominance of Ken Jennings on game show *Jeopardy*, IBM sought to create a question answering AI that could compete on the show against previous champions in another highly publicized challenge.

Watson began development in 2005 and competed against top *Jeopardy!* champions Ken Jennings and Brad Rutter in 2011. Watson won both exhibition matches, with a total score of $77,147 to Jennings' second place of $24,000.

Although it occurred a few years before the current rise in AI's popularity, Watson can be considered a harbinger of that rise. It was the first highly public example of AI outperforming humans in an unstructured domain (understanding and answering questions), the hallmark of the current AI boom fueled by deep learning.

IBM sought to capitalize on the publicity of its victory by releasing a Watson-branded commercial platform of intelligence capabilities, though it struggled to adapt its software to specific commercial use cases. Today, IBM's Watson platform bears virtually no resemblance to the *Jeopardy!* competitor. It did, however, provide a template for a generalized intelligence platform, which has since been copied by many other major technology companies (Microsoft, Google, etc.).

Netflix Prize

In 2006, Netflix launched a public competition to improve on its algorithm for predicting how a given user would rate a given movie. The company used its model as the baseline and promised a $1 million prize to whomever could achieve a 10% improvement. The prize was won in 2009 by a diverse team that had banded together with varying approaches.

The Netflix Prize is interesting for several reasons. First, it illustrated the value that companies placed on improving the intelligence of their software. While $1 million is a very small fraction of the investment that top tech companies place in advancing AI today, it was not obvious at the time that pursuing AI research was a lucrative career.

The Netflix Prize made it publicly clear that the best approach on a static dataset tended by an ensemble: a diverse set of models that could be brought to bear based on the characteristics of the individual prediction being made. This approach evolved substantially over the course of the competition, with the ultimate winners being a combination of simpler approaches that had been tried in previous years.

The Netflix Prize also established the precedent for open data science competitions, a mindset that was formalized in the Kaggle platform. Kaggle is an open data science competition platform that has seen hundreds of competitions, millions of dollars in prizes, and over a million users.

Siri

In addition to Watson, 2011 saw the advent of a second harbinger of the coming AI wave. Apple released Siri packaged with the iPhone 4S in October 2011. Originally released as an app for the iPhone in 2010 before being acquired by Apple, Siri was a voice-controlled digital assistant.

For most people, Siri was their first exposure to voice-to-text technology. Although the technology had existed for decades, the quality had traditionally been frustratingly low and had not typically been packaged into a broader useful application.

While adoption of Siri beyond novelty or entertainment remained low for years, the application showed the world what might be possible in the realm of AI assistants. Misunderstandings and lacking functionality were common in early years, but gradually diminished as companies recognized the demand for AI assistants and began investing in the underlying technology.

Siri served as inspiration for a whole ecosystem of digital assistants today, including Cortana, Google Now, and Alexa. A little over a third of millennials in the U.S. report they use a digital assistant on a regular basis[22].

Kiva Robotics

Kiva Robotics was founded in 2003 to automate material handling and fulfillment in warehouses. The company was bought by Amazon in 2012 for $775 million.

While automation in manufacturing and warehousing environments had been steadily progressing for decades, Kiva represented a public example of a new type of automation, which could better integrate into existing warehouse infrastructures and better interface with human operators.

Before Kiva, the majority of industrial robots were stationary arms that could manipulate objects immediately adjacent to them only in highly route ways. Kiva built a more mobile robot: it is squat and fits under specialized pallets full of goods. It can lift the pallets and transport them around a warehouse, with great flexibility in routing and navigation.

Kiva Robotics was renamed to Amazon Robotics in 2015. Although the company doesn't regularly report on the size of its fleet, it is estimated[23] that it had over 100,000 robots by the end of 2017.

Google search

Google is one of the most commonly used AI applications—and also probably the most commonly dismissed. While the inner workings of Google's search algorithms are constantly changing and the company is notoriously tight-lipped about how they work, enough information has been released to know that Google today uses a substantial amount of machine learning and other AI techniques to generate high quality results.

Google's AI determines the overall "rank" of a page, its relevance in given contexts, and what a user is really searching for. Google was a pioneer of "semantic search": understanding what the user is searching for, rather than just looking up results based on the keywords provided.

Google search is a prime example of how we are all using AI on a daily basis, but many people refuse to acknowledge that it is AI at all (despite not having any understanding of how it works). This is a great example of the AI Effect (the phenomenon that people tend to define AI by their familiarity with it, not by its capabilities).

Google/Facebook/Bing translation

One of the clearest radical advancements in AI technology in the most recent AI surge is machine translation. While software for translating languages has been around for years, the translations were historically awkward and often unintelligible. The past few years have seen a step-change improvement, with controlled tests yielding better-than-human results.

These more advanced AI-driven translation services have begun to be integrated into the standard internet browsing experience. Google has built translation into its Chrome browser, allowing virtually any website to be rendered in English (or the native language of the user). Facebook automatically translates its posts. Twitter automatically translates its tweets (using Microsoft's Bing service).

This new generation of language translation is another great example of people taking advanced AI for granted. Virtually everyone has come across this new intelligence, but relatively few can bring it to mind when trying to think about how AI has impacted them.

More advanced translation has opened up international communication to an extent never before known. The implications of this wider aperture of knowledge sharing have not yet been understood.

Tesla Autopilot

As of writing in mid 2019, Tesla has the most advanced autonomous capabilities available in a consumer vehicle. Tesla's autopilot offering was first launched in 2014. Its primary features include the ability to maintain a lane, accelerate and brake, and park autonomously.

While there are dozens of companies pursuing autonomous vehicle technology, Tesla provides the most available—and therefore most recognized—benchmark for progress. Since release, Tesla has been at "Level 3" autonomy: taking over control of the vehicle in limited circumstances and notifying the driver when they must take back control. They have been one of the most aggressive companies in announcing a "Level 4" timeline (vehicle can navigate the full trip autonomously), with predictions currently set for a demonstration in the next six months (the company's original prediction was for a 2017 demonstration).

Tesla has had the most public accidents of any autonomous technology, in large part due to its availability. There have been at least 4 major crashes of Tesla vehicles engaged in autopilot, with at least 2 fatalities. These incidents have proven a litmus test for society's reaction to autonomous vehicle accidents and deaths: while the events have garnered media and public attention, there has not been a general cry to stop the development or release of the technology. The events have been thoroughly investigated by the appropriate governing bodies (NHTSA, NTSB, other law enforcement agencies).

Tesla has provided early evidence that even nascent autonomous technology can provide significant reductions in motor vehicle accidents[24], and there's anecdotal evidence that its technology is less safe than some of the players who have plans to launch Level 4 autonomous vehicles in the coming years.

ImageNet

ImageNet is a database of over 14 million pictures with annotations (describing the contents of the picture, for instance). Starting in 2010, the database was the subject of an annual competition for AI models to identify the objects in the pictures.

In 2015, ImageNet helped spark the current surge in AI when researchers achieved better-than-human accuracy for the first time. When the competition started in 2010, the winner only correctly identified 72% of the images. By 2015, the winner exceeded the human rate of about 95% accuracy.

Although there were signs that AI was now a real solution for unstructured data prior to 2015, the ImageNet success spurred a tidal wave of interest in using deep neural networks for a wide variety of natural language, audio, and sound processing problems.

2017 marked the last year of the ImageNet challenge, as the "perfect" answer for the dataset had essentially been reached. There are plans for an adaptation of the challenge with a more complex problem. ImageNet gave rise to a greater interest in standardized benchmarks for measuring AI progress. Several such benchmarks have been proposed, with tasks ranging from sentence completion and question answering to scene description of images (objects plus their relationships and actions).

DeepMind - AlphaGo

DeepMind, founded in 2010, originally developed a deep learning approach to playing Atari video games. The company was bought in 2014 by Google for about $500 million based on that capability.

Shortly thereafter, DeepMind turned its attention to the game of Go, a strategic board game popular in east Asia. Go was widely considered to be the next great hurdle for AI after Deep Blue's victory over Kasparov in the game of chess. Just a year after its acquisition, DeepMind's AlphaGo software defeated the European Go champion, laying the stage for it to tackle the game's top players.

In early 2016, AlphaGo defeated Lee Sedol, considered one of the greatest Go players ever, in a 4-1 victory. While Lee Sedol was not the highest ranked player at the time, AlphaGo would go on to defeat the top ranked player in 2017.

In some ways, AlphaGo's "conquering" of the game of Go was an even more catalyzing event than AI conquering chess, even though the game did not play much of a role in western society. AlphaGo did not suffer from the same "brute force" criticisms that had been levied against Deep Blue: its deep reinforcement learning approach is widely considered to be "real" AI. Also, AI's domination of the game of Go was still widely believed to be at least a decade away, even just months before AlphaGo's victory over Lee Sedol.

DeepMind - AlphaZero

In just a couple of short years, DeepMind substantially improved on its AlphaGo software. Where AlphaGo had been trained on millions of previous human players' moves, AlphaZero started from scratch and learned by playing against itself.

In 2017, AlphaZero defeated the AlphaGo system in every one of 100 test games, using even less processing power than its predecessor. AlphaZero is also much more adaptable, and currently (as of June 2018) is the top player in the world across Go, chess, and shogi.

DeepMind - Google data centers

One criticism of DeepMind's achievements is that progress on games is irrelevant to the "real" world. These concerns were cut somewhat short in the summer of 2016 when Google announced that DeepMind's technology had been turned on its down data centers.

DeepMind had resulted in a reduction of the data centers' cooling costs by as much as 40%, a remarkable amount given that cooling makes up one of the largest costs of data center operations and Google had already been known for its efficiency.

While the results were more illustrative than a full-blown commercial case study, the savings spread across the entirety of Google's operations would represent about $400 million in annual cooling cost reductions.

The general concern that DeepMind's technology is difficult to adapt to commercial applications is a real one: today's commercial AI is still dominated by supervised learning, not reinforcement learning. Still, the DeepMind data center case study provides a compelling example of how the impact of advanced AI can be substantial when applied in the right way.

"Conquered" AI Problems

Chess

IBM's Deep Blue defeated world champion Garry Kasparov in 1997.

Go

Google DeepMind's AlphaGo defeated Lee Sedol in 2016 and world top-ranked Ke Jie in 2017.

Dota2

The OpenAI Five bot system defeated the world's top competitive sports teams in the video game Dota2 in early 2019. This marks the first time that AI has been competitive with top human players at a strategic modern video game.

Factual question answering

IBM's Watson demonstrated superhuman capabilities on question answering in 2011, at least in the specific format of its *Jeopardy!* exhibition. As of early 2018, AI models are also outperforming a human benchmark on the SQuAD dataset[25], which is intended to measure reading comprehension by having the subject answer questions about text passages.

Voice-to-text

While it has not been officially confirmed by third parties, Microsoft[26] and Baidu both claim to have AI that can convert voice into text with greater accuracy than human transcribers. This technology has seen marked improvement in the past few years; even if these specific claims prove too limited for real-world application, voice-to-text is likely at least on the cusp of being a "solved" problem for AI.

Text-to-voice

As of the end of 2017, Google has announced that its Tacotron 2 voice synthesizer is generating speech based on text, with at-human-level quality. Specifically, Google's model generates a 4.53 MOS score, compared to the marginally higher 4.58 for professionally recorded speech.

Object recognition in images

In 2015, AI surpassed a human benchmark on the ImageNet object recognition challenge. Although the real-world applicability of the models developed on this dataset are limited, the general technology has also improved substantially in the past few years.

Facial recognition

In 2015, Google FaceNet achieved 99.6% accuracy on the Labeled Faces in the Wild dataset (determining if two pictures of faces are the same person, a task that humans can perform at ~97.5% accuracy).

Medical diagnostic imaging

In the past few years, deep learning powered AI systems have outperformed trained physicians on medical diagnostic imaging in several one-off tests. The diagnostics have included pneumonia, skin cancer, and breast cancer.

Miscellaneous Lists

Top Corporations Applying AI

Google / DeepMind
Google is arguably the most advanced AI practitioner in the world. It is known in particular for its Google Brain and DeepMind groups, both of which regularly publish industry-leading research papers. AI suffuses most of Google's products: search, ads, Google Now, autonomous vehicles.

Microsoft
Microsoft is a top practitioner and AI research firm. Its cutting edge work has traditionally focused on natural language processing applications, such as voice-to-text and machine translation. As with the other major cloud providers, it has a substantial offering of cloud-based AI services.

IBM
IBM was an early advocate of the power of AI to work with unstructured data, under its Watson brand. It has lost momentum versus other top tech giants since first launching the brand in the early 2010s. IBM has seen the most success in the healthcare industry.

Facebook
Although Facebook has not pushed AI as generally as some of the other tech giants, it has achieved near-best-in-class performance in facial recognition and machine translation. It is

also well known for its intelligent ad work and timeline customization.

Amazon

Amazon was an early pioneer of product recommendation engines and remains one of the top implementers of such systems today. Amazon has also cultivated a broader set of capabilities in AI, including as a part of its cloud machine learning offering.

Uber

Uber is known for applying a variety of advanced software tools to improve their operations (ride routing, driver selection, etc.). They have a fairly large data science organization dedicated to operational efficiency. However, as of mid 2018 they're best known for their AI work in autonomous vehicles.

Uber has very publicly stated that they intend to pioneer driverless car technology, potentially eliminating the human driver component of their service over time. Over the past couple of years, they have been testing their own proprietary driverless technology on public roads. Very recently, their technology had a massive failure, striking and killing a woman crossing the street: the first instance of driverless car technology killing a pedestrian. Since the incident, Uber has placed their autonomous vehicle efforts on hold and is reportedly in talks with other technology providers.

Netflix

Netflix was an early innovator of recommendations systems, driving its movie and show recommendations for users. It also pioneered the open innovation challenge to get the community involved in improving its algorithms. Netflix's cutting-edge AI work has been more muted in recent years.

Top Academics

Andrew Ng

Andrew Ng has become best known for his online lectures as a part of Coursera's introductory course to machine learning. Ng's lectures achieved massive international popularity and actually led to his co-founding of Coursera.

Throughout his career, Andrew Ng has variously founded Google Brain, led Baidu's AI research, been the head of the AI lab at Stanford, and founded various AI focused startups and investment funds.

Yann LeCun

Yann LeCun is a French-American professor credited with the development of convolutional neural networks and popularizing deep neural networks overall. He pioneered human-level OCR in the late 80s and early 90s. Today, LeCun is affiliated with NYU and is head of AI at Facebook.

Stuart Russell

Stuart Russell is a professor associated with UC Berkeley. He is best known for co-writing *Artificial Intelligence: A Modern Approach.*

Yoshua Bengio

Yoshua Bengio is a Canadian researcher credited as being one of the main developers of deep learning (along with Yann LeCun and Geoffrey Hinton). He is affiliated with the University of Montreal and co-founded Element AI, a well-funded AI consultancy.

Fei-Fei Li

Fei-Fei Li is a Stanford-affiliated researcher, known for her work in image recognition and advocating for more diversity in the field. She is perhaps best known for her leadership role on ImageNet, a competition that contributed to the rise of the modern AI revolution.

Ian Goodfellow

Ian Goodfellow is a relatively young AI engineer who has achieved notoriety by inventing GANs. He has worked at

Google Brain and OpenAI and now is a leader in Apple's AI group.

Geoffrey Hinton

Geoffrey Hinton is a Canadian AI researcher famous for developing the backpropagation training method that enabled the rise of deep learning. He is affiliated with the University of Toronto and Google Brain.

Further Resources

"The AI Revolution: The Road to Superintelligence" on *Wait But Why* - A very long, two-part blog post exploring the potential for AI to impact society. Helped contribute to the start of the AI revolution in 2015.

Andreessen Horowitz AI Playbook - A hands-on website exploring various basic AI technologies. .

Coursera Machine Learning course - Andrew Ng's lectures out of Stanford, which drove the development of Coursera and contributed to the rise of MOOCs.

Fast.ai Practical Deep Learning for Coders - A relatively new online course teaching deep learning.

Artificial Intelligence: A Modern Approach - Considered by many to be the "bible" of AI, this textbook by Stuart Russell and Peter Norvig is used in many university-level AI courses.

The Singularity is Near - A popular book in which futurologist Ray Kurzweil explore the long-term potential of AI. The book is a bit dated at this point, but still has value as an optimistic exploration of what AI might enable in society.

Superintelligence - The spiritual counterpoint to *The Singularity is Near*, in which Nick Bostrom details the potential dangers of

AI that gets too smart, as well as laying out tactical steps for preventing a disaster scenario.

Rise of the Robots - A popular book in the business community about the potential for automation and AI to displace human workers.

References

1. "Artificial Intelligence - The Next Digital Frontier?" by McKinsey Global Institute. Accessed Dec. 2017
2. "Artificial intelligence", Merriam Webster. Accessed online Dec. 2017.
3. "Adages and Coinages" by Larry Tesler. Accessed from nomodes.com in Dec. 2017.
4. Russell, Stuart J.; Norvig, Peter (2003), Artificial Intelligence: A Modern Approach (2nd ed.), Upper Saddle River, New Jersey: Prentice Hall, ISBN 0-13-790395-2
5. "Heuristic Problem Solving: The Next Advance in Operations Research" Herbert A. Simon and Allen Newell. 1958. Intermediate source: "What should we learn from past AI forecasts?" published by the Open Philanthropy Project. Accessed Dec. 2017.
6. "Speculations on Perceptrons and Other Automata" I. J. Good. 1959. Intermediate source: "What should we learn from past AI forecasts?" published by the Open Philanthropy Project. Accessed Dec. 2017.
7. *Computers and the World of the Future*. Edited by Martin Greenberger. Intermediate source: "What should we learn from past AI forecasts?" published by the Open Philanthropy Project. Accessed Dec. 2017.
8. "A New Robot Density Must Track Global Robotics Growth" by Abishur Prakash in *Robotics Business Review*. September 11, 2016.
9. "Why work? A psychologist explains the deeper meaning of your daily grind" by Anne Quito in *Quartz*. September 15, 2015.

10. "How Much Did a Shirt Really Cost in the Middle Ages?" by Sean Manning. Accessed from bookandsword.com. December 9, 2017.

11. "How We're Predicting AI—or Failing To" by Stuart Armstrong and Kaj Sotala. Accessed from intelligence.org on September 2, 2018.

12. I could not find a good comprehensive source for the increase in DNN sizes over time, but it is generally accepted that the capabilities of today's cutting-edge networks with dozens of hidden layers exceed those of substantially smaller networks in decades past. For a relatively recent exploration of network size increases, and related architectures/results, see "Deep Residual Learning for Image Recognition" by Kaiming He, et. al. Accessed from arxiv.org. December 10, 2015.

13. "Meet The Man Who Lives Normally With Damage to 90% of His Brain" by Fiona MacDonald. Accessed from sciencealert.com. July 13, 2016.

14. "New AI can work out whether you're gay or straight from a photograph" by Sam Levin in *The Guardian.* September 7, 2017.

15. "A machine learning predictor of facial attractiveness revealing human-like psychophysical biases" by Amit Kagian, et. al. Accessed from sciencedirect.com. January 2008.

16. "UK police use of facial recognition technology a failure, says report" by Vikram Dodd in *The Guardian.* May 14, 2018.

17. "Results from the 2016 national survey on drug use and health: detailed tables" from the Substance Abuse and Mental Health Services Administration, Center for Behavioral Health Statistics and Quality. September 7, 2017.

18. "Machine Bias" by Julia Angwin, Jeff Larson, Surya Mattu and Lauren Kirchner in *ProPublica.* May 23, 2016.

19. "AI Perpetuating Human Bias In The Lending Space" by Ernest Hamilton in *Tech Times.* April 2, 2019.

20. "NYC students take aim at segregation by hacking an algorithm" by Jay Cassano in *Fast Company.* April 16, 2019.

21. "Discriminating Systems: Gender, Race, and Power in AI" by Sarah Myers West, Meredith Whittaker, and Kate Crawford. AI Now Institute. April 2019.
22. "Voice-Activated Digital Assistant Adoption" by David Erickson at *MarketingCharts.com*. June 15, 2017.
23. "There are 170,000 fewer retail jobs in 2017—and 75,000 more Amazon robots" by Dave Edwards and Helen Edwards in *Quartz*. December 4, 2017.
24. "Tesla Says Autopilot is Statistically Safer Than a Human Driver" by Kristin Houser in *Futurism*. April 10, 2019.
25. Performance on the SQuAD dataset can be found at https://rajpurkar.github.io/SQuAD-explorer/
26. "Microsoft's voice-recognition tech is now better than even teams of humans at transcribing conversations" by Matt Weinberger in *Business Insider*. August 21, 2017.

Made in the USA
San Bernardino, CA
19 December 2019